Planning and the Market in the U.S.S.R.: The 1960's

Planning and the Market in the U.S.S.R.: The 1960's

Alexander Balinky *Abram Bergson*

John N. Hazard *Peter Wiles*

RUTGERS UNIVERSITY PRESS

NEW BRUNSWICK, NEW JERSEY

Library of Congress Catalogue Number: 67–16277
Manufactured in the United States of America by
H. Wolff Book Manufacturing Co., Inc., New York

Preface

This work has as its general objective an investigation into the nature and the implications of the Soviet economic reforms of the 1960's. As Abram Bergson states in the opening of Chapter II, these "recently announced decisions of the Soviet government to reform its planning system have been greeted in the West as a momentous international event."

Each of the contributors has agreed to assume responsibility for a distinct focus in regard to this subject as well as to write for a wider audience than that of the Soviet specialist or professional economist. Chapter I, therefore, is designed to offer the historical-ideological and technical background to the current economic reforms as well as to pose some of the issues and problems involved therein. Chapter II sets forth the specific character of the planning reforms, assesses their significance, and offers some hints as to the direction the economy of the Soviet Union is likely to take in the near future. Chapter III examines the relationship between such economic reforms and Soviet politics, for as its author, John N. Hazard, points out, "economic policy is closely associated with political consequences in the minds of Soviet leaders." Chapter IV by Peter Wiles raises the long-term issue of the possible convergence of East-West economies. These are, to be sure, closely related areas of inquiry, and some overlap is to be expected. Differences in viewpoint among the four contributors to this volume fairly represent the character of the controversy on this subject as it exists within the profession.

This book owes its origin to a symposium, "Is the Soviet Economy Moving toward Capitalism?", which was held on April 13, 1966, at Rutgers University. Professors Abram Bergson, John N. Hazard, and Peter Wiles were the participants and I served as moderator. The symposium was under the sponsorship of the Rutgers Russian Area Committee and the Rutgers Economics Honor Society. The sponsors are indebted to Student Council and the New Brunswick College of Arts and Sciences for making the necessary funds available. Great appreciation is due to the following people who were instrumental in making both the symposium and this book possible: Monroe Berkowitz, Chairman of the Department of Economics, College of Arts and Sciences in New Brunswick; Arnold Grobman, Dean of the College of Arts and Sciences in New Brunswick; Ernest Lynton, Dean of Livingston College.

Alexander Balinky

September, 1966
New Brunswick, New Jersey

Contents

Planning and the Market in the U.S.S.R.: The 1960's

I

Problems and Issues in Soviet Economic Reform

Alexander Balinky

Western thought has never been entirely free of theories or myths about the self-destructive propensities of Soviet society. Varying in sophistication, duration, and currency, several of these theories have already been exploded, some persist, and another may well be in the making. A brief reference to some of the most prominent of these theories will serve to place the issue of the current Soviet economic reforms in historical perspective.

Following the October, 1917, Revolution, a general optimism prevailed in the West that the Bolshevik regime would not survive the near chaos, post-

Revolutionary expectation, starvation, and organized resistance as well as intervention that characterized the period of War Communism. Western optimism was rekindled in 1921 and 1922 when Lenin was forced to take "one step backward" under the New Economic Policy. The view then current in the West was that socialism had lost out and capitalism was about to emerge triumphant in Russia. This conclusion was shared even by certain Marxists, but they reached it along a somewhat different path of reasoning. The argument put forth by such Marxists was that since the logic of Marxian economics calls first for a fully mature capitalism, socialism could hardly be expected to take root in Russia's semifeudal soil.

During the period of the Stalinist Five-Year Plans (1928 to 1941) alternative theories emerged. The early and positive assessment of Russia's socialist economy by Beatrice and Sidney Webb and the one by Lincoln Steffens—"I have seen the future and it works"—most certainly constituted a minority view. The Soviets were still in the throes of the First Five-Year Plan when the American journalist and muckraker Lincoln Steffens, on his return from the U.S.S.R., made this famous pronouncement. Beatrice and Sidney Webb, well-known Fabian socialists, came to much the same conclusion in 1934. But the dominant conviction was that Soviet socialism was not working and, indeed, could not be made to work. More than three decades passed before the main body of disputants came to appreciate, at least fully, the essential irrelevancy of the issue as it had been formulated and argued during most of the period from 1928 to 1941. The relevant question, as serious students of Soviet affairs now agree, is not whether the Soviet economy has worked or can work, but how well and in relation to what and whose goals.

Nevertheless, numerous theoretical arguments, at various levels of analytic complexity, were offered by Western economists in support of the view that predominated from 1928 to 1941. Only the barest elements involved in their reasoning can be mentioned here. The main point was that a planned economy by its very nature is incapable of solving the fundamental problem common to all economic systems, namely the rational allocation of scarce resources in relation to the maximization of consumer satisfaction. Second, the cost of planning in terms of resource utilization, bureaucratic waste, second and third order effects, etc., was declared inordinately high. Third, unfree labor would have little incentive to productivity. The strongest defense of this position is to be found in the works of such Western economists as Ludwig von Mises and Frederick Hayek. The more modern and more sophisticated version is well represented in the writings of Milton Freedman and his followers.

Concurrently, the notion that a totalitarian regime is basically unstable, doomed to destroy itself from within, has also sunk deep roots in Western consciousness. A variety of assurances had been offered here. Some lost their point with the end of the Stalinist epoch, but others have since taken their place. A familiar view prior to 1953 was that a tyrant can only push the people to a point where they have very little to lose and that Stalin had about reached that limit. Another was that a struggle for power among the members of the ruling oligarchy was inevitable and would eventuate in the collapse of the Bolshevik regime. The popularity of these two notions reached an apex just before and after Stalin's death and waned rapidly as Nikita Khrushchev consolidated his position.

With the shift from Stalinist coercion to Khrushchevian persuasion a different set of hypotheses gained in appeal. When people are given a modicum of freedom, be it economic, political, or intellectual, they begin to expect and finally to clamor for more. Who knows where this can end? A related expectation is that the same brilliant minds responsible for Russian scientific and technical progress will, as they must, turn to questioning the philosophical and political basis of communist society. A current theory is that various groups or sub-classes within Soviet society—the military, the industrial-managerial class, the intelligentsia, for instance—are emerging as independent *vis-à-vis* the Party. The presumption here is that such groups seek to preserve the *status quo* or have ends that are at variance with Bolshevik ideology or Communist imperialism. This is to say nothing about the hope that has been generated by the Sino-Soviet conflict, the emergence of polycentrism in the Communist world, and many other possible sources of optimism as viewed from the West.

A current source of optimism stems from the economic reforms that are being instituted or are under consideration in the U.S.S.R. The main point at issue here is whether these reforms are, in fact, altering the basic character of the Soviet economy from socialism to capitalism. I have purposely stated this proposition in its most general and obvious form at this point. This is done, in part, in order to underline the form in which this proposition has found expression in the popular mind. Another, more cogent, reason will become apparent later in this chapter.

This brings us to the first of several related questions with which this volume is directly concerned. (1) Why has the view that the Soviet economy is moving in the direction of capitalism become so widely accepted in the West? The force with which Soviet economists and official Soviet spokesmen deny that these reforms constitute a move toward capitalism attests to the popularity of this view in the West. (2) Does the evidence, as examined and interpreted by the authors of this volume, warrant this conclusion? Is there, in other words, a realistic basis for the prevailing optimism? (3) Or is this conclusion, like some of the notions mentioned earlier, just another myth based on little more than the will to believe?

Suppose, for the moment, that these economic reforms are leading the Russians toward capitalism. There remains the problem of isolating the real from the fancied reasons why this may be so. The extent to which the popular basis for existing optimism is tinged with elements of fancy, as the reader will see, makes this distinction relevant. Four sets of terms or concepts stand out in the literature on the current Soviet economic reforms: (1) profit, profit rate, profit motive, profit system; (2) bonuses, premium pay, income differentials; (3) consumer sovereignty, freedom, choice, preference, satisfaction; (4) decentralization, local initiative. The proposition as stated above would, indeed, be correct by adding one further assumption: that the economic reforms in question actually involve the introduction of or greater reliance on these four sets of concepts as understood or conventionally used in Western economics.

It is with this second assumption that special problems arise. One is that Soviet economists use many of the same words or terms but mean something quite different by them. Another is that some of the words within each category are not necessarily synonyms even in Western usage. A third problem, of a different order, is the persistence in the West of some common misconceptions or lack of familiarity with Marxist-Leninist doctrine as it relates to the current Soviet economic reforms. Since these appear to be the three main elements entering into the unwarranted side of Western optimism in connection with the Soviet economic reforms, they call for some detailed comment and illustration.

Because so much is heard these days about the role of profit and its growing importance in the Soviet economy, this category will be considered first. Soviet economists use this word in two different contexts: in its historical or Marxian sense, as a synonym for surplus value and thus in particular reference to capitalist economies; and in a technical sense, as an instrument of planning and control and therefore as a socialist phenomenon. Profit in the latter sense is defined by a Soviet source as "a method of planned operations of socialist enterprises which requires the carrying out of state-determined tasks . . . by the ensuring of profitability of enterprises."[1] Our concern here is with this meaning, which, thus far at least, has had only a tenuous connection with the Western concept of profit or the role that profit plays in a market-oriented economy. The possibility that profit may some day play an analogous role in the Soviet economy is a point which will be considered. For the present a brief, and thus necessarily oversimplified, account of the nature of Soviet profit in its technical sense will help to clarify the issue under consideration.

The use of profit as a planning and control device dates back to the time of the First Five-Year Plan. By 1929 nearly all state enterprises had been accorded the status of autonomous financial entities and placed on a system of ruble control called *khozraschyot* (economic accounting). Since by definition a state enterprise is state owned and operated, its long-term capital requirements are met directly out of the All-Union budget. That is to say, an enterprise is not charged interest either on its starting capital or (with some exceptions) on the capital required for major modernization, expansion of scale, and the like. The managerial-entrepreneurial function within the enterprise is performed by the director and such principal aides as his chief accountant, production engineer, etc. An enterprise is required, however, to record its current transactions (its purchases and sales) in a special set of accounts. The primary purpose of this system is to enable all concerned to ascertain the extent to which an enterprise has operated at a profit or loss during a given time period.

Very briefly, without the changes that the current economic reforms would bring about, the system works as follows. Central authority sets three principal constraints within which the enterprise must operate. There is, first, an output plan. Actually an enterprise may be assigned several kinds of plans. Depending on the nature of the operations, such plans are expressed in physical units, value terms, and so on. Significant variations exist in the extent to which Central authority specifies such further details as design, style of product, quality, product mix, etc. A complex system of up-and-down-the-line communication and bargaining, involving the Economic Ministries (to 1958 and now again), the Central Planning Agency (Gosplan), and the enterprises occurs. Finally, however, the plan targets are officially assigned to the enterprises. Second, an enterprise is given a schedule of input and output prices. Third, the system involves the use of allocation certificates without which the basic and scarcer inputs cannot be procured. It is not possible here to enter into a discussion of the supply plan, allocation certificates, funded, unfunded and planned inputs.[2] All that need be said for the point at hand is that the allocation of such certificates is determined at a level above that of the enterprise (but not without some bargaining), with priorities reflecting the requirements of the All-Union plan.

Given these constraints, the function of the enterprise director and his staff is to fulfill or, if possible or desirable, exceed the assigned plans as cheaply as possible in terms of resource utilization. The performance of an enterprise is assessed in two ways. It is measured in terms of one or more specific success indicators such as physical output, labor productivity, cost reduction, the saving of a critically short input, or a variety of other indicators peculiar to an enterprise's operations. Enterprise performance is also measured by a general index, that of its profitability. The following account should clarify the special or technical sense in which this term is used by the Soviets. The system whereby enterprises are required to pay for their inputs and are paid for the sale of their output is made possible because each enterprise has something called an operating capital fund. Enterprises enter into contractual relationships with one another, and such contracts have the force of law.

All expenditures and receipts by an enterprise are recorded in a set of accounts from which a profit and loss statement is derived. Most purchases and sales are really recorded in terms of accounting rubles, with special provision being made for the payment of wages and salaries. The Central Bank (Gosbank) keeps a corresponding set of accounts for the economy as a whole.

An enterprise is said to show a profit if at the close of the plan year total receipts exceed total expenditures in this accounting sense. But the matter is not quite that simple. Enterprise profit is made up of two components: planned and over-plan profit. In regard to the former, enterprises operate on the basis of a financial plan that is tied in with output and all other plans. This financial plan includes a centrally determined planned profit for the enterprise in question. It could also be a planned loss in those cases where Central authority sees the necessity or wishes to subsidize a particular form of production, an industry, or an enterprise. Theoretically, planned profit represents the difference between an enterprise's total cost and revenue which should appear if that enterprise operates at the level of efficiency anticipated or planned by Central authority. The rationale here, and behind varying the rate of planned profit among the enterprises, is the recognition by Central authority that some enterprises have locational, natural, or capital advantages over others.

Over-plan profit reflects the extent to which an enterprise succeeds in attaining a level of efficiency, that is, cost reduction, greater than that which had been planned for or anticipated by Central authority. In real or resource terms this could take the form of overfulfilling the output plan with a given sum of inputs or just meeting the target but utilizing less of inputs than had been expected. With economic maturity the second approach is becoming preferred. In any case, it is this over-plan component of profit that is of special interest to Central authority and the general basis on which an enterprise's performance is judged.

That this is so may be seen from the nature of a related planning instrumentality known as the enterprise fund. The appropriate question at this point is, what happens to enterprise profit (planned plus over-plan) as it appears on the books of the enterprise? A portion of the total is technically taxed away, that is, transferred to the state budget. The so-called profits tax is one of a number of sources of state investment funds. Since these are state-owned units, which pay no interest on capital, there is no legal or property-rights reason why the state cannot tax away the full amount of enterprise profit. In practice and for reasons of incentive, the state permits the enterprise to retain a certain portion of such profit. What remains, therefore, constitutes the enterprise fund. It is important to note that the enterprise fund consists mainly of over-plan profits. It is difficult to generalize in this case, but on the average enterprises have been permitted to retain 2 to 4 per cent of planned profits and as much as 30 to 40 per cent of over-plan profit. Significant variations exist in both planned and over-plan percentages depending on the industry, the line of production, etc., and this, too, serves as a control device. The uses to which the enterprise may put this fund is a clear indication of the incentive factor involved in the system. According to state regulations, the enterprise fund is to be used as a means of rewarding workers for their part in the successful performance of their enterprise. The reward may be indirect and take the form of investment in the improvement of enterprise housing, the plant cafeteria, or numerous other elements that enter into conditions of employment. The direct form is the payment of bonuses, in money or in kind, to those workers whose performance has been especially meritorious. The enterprise director, with the advice and consent of the trade union local, has a considerable degree of freedom in this case. The total of this enterprise fund has traditionally, by state regulations, been held to about 5 or 6 per cent of the wages bill.

The following facts about the role of profit in the Soviet economy, therefore, deserve special emphasis. (1) It is not an innovation associated with present trends or the current economic reforms. This is not to say that the current reforms do not involve certain changes in the existing system. (2) Neither planned nor over-plan profits have involved a return to private capital. (3) Its prime purpose has been to provide Central authority with a general index of enterprise success or failure. (4) The core of its incentive feature, the enterprise fund, is linked to the performance of the workers as against the director and his chief aides. Enterprise directors and their principal aides are rewarded in ways and out of sources that lie outside the enterprise fund. Reward, in this case, is some combination of position retention or promotion, monetary bonuses, and public recognition. Of course, the opposite occurs in the event of failure. In any case, everyone, directors as well as workers, receive bonuses and the like as state employees. To say that receipt of such bonuses represents a form of profit-sharing, based on the collective ownership of Soviet factories, mines, etc., is to play with words.

In recent years there has been mounting self-criticism in the U.S.S.R. of the basis on which enterprise performance is being measured and rewarded. Current Soviet literature is replete with illustrations of ways by which enterprise directors have maneuvered so as to show success without really meeting the intended requirements of the plan or relating output to use-value. The fundamental weakness in the case of the specific success indicators is that each imparts its own peculiar bias to enterprise performance which, moreover, the existing system of rewards only tends to reinforce. A few illustrations of such bias will suffice. Primary reliance on a quantity of output index (in physical units) diverts attention from the quality of the product, its style and its variety. The unit of measurement selected may impart a further bias. Thus, to use the classic example, "number of units" would lead a nail-producing enterprise to make only the smallest nails; while "tons" would induce that same enterprise to produce the largest nails, all, of course, at the expense of some common sense mix of nails required by the economy. This type of distortion can be corrected by expressing output in monetary terms, that is, gross value of output; but, again, only at the expense of a different set of distortions. A value of output yardstick clearly encourages an enterprise to use more expensive inputs than may be technically necessary. Gross value of output offers little inducement to an enterprise to complete production, since goods in process are counted. This bias can be corrected by using value added, but only at the cost of yet another distortion. The same is true when some other than an output indicator is used. Cost reduction, for instance, introduces an opposite bias from that of gross value of output. It encourages an enterprise to use the cheapest inputs without regard to quality of product, the desired output mix, and so on. In any case cost reduction, to be meaningful, must await the solution of a far more complex problem of factor pricing. Labor productivity as a success indicator is extremely difficult to measure and is in many ways a very slippery concept. And so on.

As a consequence of the above, some Soviet economists and planners are now urging greater reliance on the general or profit indicator of enterprise performance. In this case the principal problem is that of meaningfulness. Here we may recall the three centrally determined constraints within which an enterprise operates. To what extent does the realization of over-plan profit or loss truly represent efficiency or inefficiency of enterprise performance, and to what extent is it the consequence of planning error, accident, illegal procurement practices, etc.? Since profit, as used here, is the difference between an enterprise's total cost and revenue, how good is such a measure in light of the existing inadequacy or irrationality of Soviet cost-pricing practice? Cost is all the more significant here since it is Soviet practice to express the rate of profit as a percentage of cost. The fact that enterprise cost has been exclusive of interest and rent charges is critical to this issue. The fundamental solution in this regard depends on a resolution of such questions as how factory prices can be made to reflect the real relative scarcities of resources, the relationship between average cost of production and final prices of output, what to do about the "law of value," and similar questions.

The fact remains that one important aspect of the current economic reforms does involve paying greater attention to the principle of profit maximization on the part of the Soviet enterprise; and this calls for certain changes in the existing constraints. Thus the points at issue in regard to this aspect of the economic reforms—what the reader might look for in the chapters that follow—are these: Do the current reforms involve a basic departure from the system or purpose as described here? Is there, in other words, any evidence of change in the direction of the role that profit plays in a market-oriented economy? Or is the endeavor on the part of the Soviets in this regard simply to find a more effective instrument for measuring and rewarding enterprise performance within the framework of a centrally planned socialist economy?

A second basis for Western optimism in regard to the current Soviet economic reforms has to do with the matter of bonuses, premium pay, and income differentials. The popular Western notion here may, very roughly, be set down in three propositions. (1) The Soviets regard raising the level of worker productivity to be vital in the realization of present-day economic goals. (2) Current Soviet policy, therefore, calls for even greater reliance on and certain changes in the system of premium pay and bonuses as well as a further widening of income differentials. (3) This policy represents a marked deviation from the socialist principle of incentive, reward, and distribution, and is thus further proof of convergence between East and West. The first proposition is entirely correct, and the second is reasonably so. The third, which offers a basis for optimism, is the one which most deserves to be questioned.

Those who subscribe to the third proposition do so, or so it seems to me, because of a common tendency to link profit motive to capitalism and to exclude it from the *theory* of socialism. The existence of the profit motive in the Soviet Union is, of course, readily acknowledged by Westerners, but primarily as a deviation from the socialist "ideal." Profit motive is not a synonym for profit or profit rate in either the Western or the Soviet sense, though confusion here is not unknown. The sense in which this term is used here becomes apparent in that which follows, and it is in that sense that Marxism-Leninism leaves considerable scope for its operation in a socialist, as against a communist, society.

Classic Marxist doctrine on this subject runs along the following lines. During the capitalist epoch workers labor because they must, as a condition of survival, not for the love of work or the good of society. The logic of the capitalist engine, to take a phrase from Joseph Schumpeter, drives the capitalists as well but for a different set of reasons. The capitalist must accumulate, out of surplus value, in order to survive. Given the capitalist environment, therefore, work or involvement in economic activity generates disutility which must be offset by individual, material reward. It is interesting to note, just in passing, that the notion of the wage as the price paid for the disutility of working has had a long history in Western economic thought. A significant difference between the Marxist and non-Marxist approach, however, is that the latter assumed disutility of work to be so regardless of the institutional framework. Returning to the main lines of the Marxian argument, this explains why capitalism requires that there be a direct functional relationship between worker productivity and reward. That same economic logic, moreover, is held to generate inequality of income not only between but within the two main classes. Some workers require more by way of a subsistence wage than others, some capitalists are bigger than others.

What changes in these regards will socialism bring? Marxist doctrine assures us that a break in the historical relationship between productivity and reward will inevitably occur. A time will come when everyone will work for the joy of it and the good of society and receive according to need. But not under socialism. The emergence of a socialist productive force will bring an end to the exploitation of man by man, of one class by another.[3] But only, according to Marxist-Leninist-Stalinist doctrine, after an initial period during which the "many oppress the few." The U.S.S.R. is said to have passed that stage by 1936, following the "liquidation" of the "enemies from within" and the adoption of the 1936 Constitution.

After certain necessary deductions, the total social product will then be distributed in full, but not equally or according to need. Marx set down six categories of deductions of an administrative and social welfare nature. Those who work, therefore, will be paid in relation to their productivity, "proportional to the amount of labor they contribute." Thus socialist equality is defined as "the equal obligation of all to work" and "the unequal right for unequal work" or the right of every worker to be "measured by an equal measure, labor." As Marx himself pointed out, in practice this means that under socialism one worker "will be richer than the other and so forth." [4] Lenin and the Bolsheviks did begin, early in the period of War Communism, by toying with simple equality in distribution and somewhat later with very narrow wage differentials. Post-Revolutionary expectation on the part of the mass is probably a more reasonable explanation for this policy than any misreading of Marx by Lenin on this issue.[5] Thus Marx and the Marxists clearly admit the "deficiency," the *bourgeois* character, of the socialist principle of distribution, incentive and reward; and, since the early 1930's, Stalin insisted on its fullest logical development.

The persistence of the profit motive under socialism follows from the essence of Marx's theory of history. Social change is said to occur dialectically and to originate within the productive force. Corresponding changes are reflected in the superstructure *but only with a time lag.* The change from a capitalist to a socialist productive force comes first. Institutions, attitudes, patterns of mass behavior, which, in the final analysis, take the form required by the logic of the economic base, do not immediately conform to the character of the freshly emerged productive force. Thus the mass of workers and peasants enter socialism with existing differences in education, skills, capacities, etc., as well as with a dominantly "vestigial" (*bourgeois*) attitude toward work and its reward. What the socialist state will have to contend with, wrote Marx, is a society "not as if it had *developed on a basis of its own,* but on the contrary as it *emerges from capitalist society,* which is thus in every respect tainted economically, morally and intellectually with the hereditary diseases of the old society from whose womb it is emerging." [6] This, therefore, is why the socialist state must continue, in the main, to reward workers in accordance with their productivity, in a more or less traditional manner. But since, according to that same doctrine, socialism is also a period during which the workers are expected to become more nearly equally educated and cultured, there is nothing inconsistent about the introduction of non-*bourgeois* forms of incentive and reward.

Why has proposition three become so deeply rooted in Western thought? It may well be a result of the inadequate awareness of the Marxian distinction between socialism and communism. As (neo-)

Hegelians, Marxists view history as the unfolding in six stages of the "absolute," the final, perfect, and, therefore, changeless society. The six stages of history are primitive communism, slavery, feudalism, capitalism, socialism, and full communism. Since by Marxist count socialism is only the fifth stage of social history, it represents an improvement over capitalism but is not yet the perfect social order. Perfection must await the emergence of full communism, which is the name Marxists give to the terminal social order. (This distinction between socialism as transitional and communism as terminal is, incidentally, one of the more meaningful approaches to distinguishing between Marxian or scientific socialism and all other forms of socialism such as Utopian, Fabian, etc.)

Thus, the notion that reliance by the Soviet Union on the profit motive is unsocialist may stem from the failure to separate what Marxists say must occur under socialism and what is due to occur under communism. George Orwell's witticism in *Animal Farm* that under socialism "all animals are equal but some are more equal than others" has, regrettably, only served to reinforce this common misconception. In fact, of course, Orwell meant something far more subtle.

But then Marxists must bear equal blame for generating confusion on this point. The document calling on the workers to establish a socialist society is entitled the Communist Manifesto. The Union of Soviet Socialist Republics has, as its ruling body, the Communist Party. Marx frequently referred to socialism as the lower phase of communism.

According to Marxist theory, the profit motive is due to disappear. The break in the functional relationship between productivity and reward will occur, but not until the emergence of full communism. Marx put it as follows: "In a higher phase of communist society, after the tyrannical subordination of individuals according to the distribution of labor and thereby also the distinction between manual and intellectual work, have disappeared, after labor has become not merely a means to live but in itself the first necessity of living, after the powers of production have also increased and all the springs of cooperative wealth are gushing freely together with the all-round development of the individual, then and then only can the narrow *bourgeois* horizon of rights be left far behind and society will inscribe on its banner: 'From each according to his capacity, to each according to his need.' "[7] But even here, correctly interpreted, Marxist doctrine does not have in mind equality in distribution in any ordinary sense of that term. This, however, is another matter and beyond the point at hand.[8]

The fact, therefore, that the current Soviet economic reforms involve even greater reliance than in the past on material reward, on bonus payments and premium pay, does not as such constitute a realistic basis for optimism. In regard to Soviet income differentials, no single trend is discernible. The growth of a professional income elite is undeniable. A reversal of the traditional urban-rural pattern, in favor of the peasant, is in evidence. The percentage of the social wage to total personal income has been growing. Positive answers to such questions as the following, on the other hand, would offer a sounder basis for optimism. (1) If fully operative, would these reforms result in an increase in the percentage of income to total generated in the private sector of the Soviet economy? I have in mind such elements as income earned by the so-called independent artisans, income from private law or medical practice, income from the sale of agricultural produce from private plots of land, or other private acts of trade. (2) Would these reforms enable Soviet citizens to earn incomes from sources which, at least since the end of the New Economic Policy, have been nonexistent or illegal? (3) Is there any suggestion in these reforms of a reversal in the Marxist-Leninist ranking of property or property rights, that is to say, in the status (going from the lowest to the highest stage of socialist development) of private, collective, and state property?

Embourgeoisement, the changing status of the Soviet citizen as consumer, is another widely held basis for the belief that the Russians are moving in the direction of capitalism.[9] That the Russian rulers have become increasingly concerned with the importance of raising the Soviet living standard, whatever their reasons, need not be argued. Unlike the past, however, now the focus is on the qualitative side of consumption and the means by which to attain this objective. It is in this connection that one hears a great deal about the relatively new role that consumer sovereignty (freedom, choice, preference, satisfaction) is playing in the Soviet economy. Whether this development constitutes a realistic or an illusory basis for optimism depends, in good measure, on whether preoccupation with consumer satisfaction is characteristically capitalist, as against socialist or Bolshevik, and whether consumer satisfaction or preference is quite the same as consumer freedom or sovereignty.

An answer to the first question hinges, of course, on what one assumes about human nature and behavior, an area into which the economist or Soviet specialist best tread lightly. Albert Parry, for instance, rests his case about the *embourgeoisement* of Soviet society on a single premise. The problem, he tells us, "is that things material do become paramount with the middle-and-upper-class man and his family in the Soviet Union. . . . With comforts and conveniences, with elevated stations in life, emerges a new psychology quite at variance with the stern Marxist-Leninist precepts. Not only in the fact of his possessions of worldly goods and social prestige, but even more in the attitude to this possession, the new elite man is indeed bourgeois. For his attitude is that the possession and its enjoyment is an aim in itself, not a mere unstressable consequence of his progress." [10] The specific nature of Albert Parry's premise, as well as its weakness, is brought out by Eli Ginzberg in a recent article on the relationship of psychology to economics. Ginzberg writes: "It became clear early to me that most economic theory has an implicit or explicit psychological foundation; the most prevalent variant is a rationalistic, hedonistic view of man which can be summarized by saying that there is a Scotsman inside each of us. Since the Benthamite psychology, even in its modern dress, seemed to me to be too gross, I wanted to seek for more perceptive and relevant theories of human behavior." [11] Present-day Soviet preoccupation with the material side of life may surely transform Soviet society in the Western image, but only if Parry's premise about human nature happens to be the correct one and if the Soviet people can find the political or other means by which to force the Soviet rulers to conform to their wishes in areas that really matter.

Starting with the works of Karl Marx and ending with the official pronouncements of Leonid Brezhnev and Alexsei Kosygin, one point in this same connection seems clear enough. There is no inconsistency between striving for or the attainment of material improvement and Marxist-Leninist ideology. According to this doctrine, the very logic of a socialist economy *finally* assures all the people a material standard far in excess of that attainable under capitalism. The word *finally* is added in recognition of that part of the doctrine which admits of a time lag in surpassing the level of production under capitalism. The time lag is said to be due to special historical circumstances, the vestigialness of the mass, capitalist encirclement, obstruction by internal class enemies, etc. The higher living standard ultimately attainable is also held to be a function of the superiority of the socialist system of distribution as well as production. Indeed, an economy of abundance (defined as enough of everything to meet fully the needs of cultured human beings) is regarded as a precondition for the development of the so-called perfect collectivist man; which, in turn and with certain other conditions, is a requisite for entry into full communism.

There are two respects, according to Marxist-Leninist theory, in which even a socialist economy does not at first, or for some time to come, fully satisfy the needs and desires of the consumer. There are, first, innumerable obstacles that must be overcome before the logical superiority of a socialist economy can manifest itself. The administrative and planning apparatus of a socialist society must be organized, planning theory developed, people trained, and so on. In the case of Russia, it was added, industrialization must first occur. Thus, there is a period when everyone will have to do with less of most things than is needed. The second respect is more directly to the point under discussion. Since the majority is said to enter socialism and to remain for some time in a state of vestigialness, the power to decide on what kinds of consumer goods and services to produce must reside with the Party. To the extent, therefore, that the citizenry continues to desire items that are deemed by the Party to be unnecessary, wasteful, or reflective of *bourgeois* decadence, consumer satisfaction is purposefully not met.

But two endogenous forces are also said to be operating throughout the period of socialist construction. Obstacles to the attainment of a high order of production are gradually surmounted. At the same time, life and work in a socialist economic environment causes a gradual transformation in the attitudes and behavior patterns of the people. *Bourgeois* attitudes and behavior give way to "socialist consciousness." Thus both gaps narrow over the course of socialist development. The general living standard is said to rise and every effort is bent to produce that which is most desired by the progressively less vestigial, more socialist-conscious consumers. Consumer freedom, then, is like political or any other freedom. For a person is only truly free, according to Marxist-Leninist doctrine, when he does or wants that which is historically necessary. So much for Marxist ideology on this point.

The crucial question here is whether the current Soviet economic reforms really involve the emergence of consumer freedom or sovereignty in a non-Marxian sense or as commonly understood in the West. The traditional Soviet approach has been to regard all items of consumption as imbued with either an ideological, practical, or neutral content. By ideological content I mean a case where the Party has consistently refused to permit the allocation of resources for the publication of, say, Western-style comics and has severely limited the availability of resources for the printing of Bibles; at the same time being extremely generous in regard to the flow of resources for the publication of works by Marx,

Engels, and Lenin. By practical content I mean the purposeful restriction in the assortment of goods, colors, styles, etc., at a time when all items of consumption are in short supply. Such restrictions, as in the case of cosmetics, had been given an overlay of ideology from which it is relatively easy to depart. By neutral content I mean a case where, for example, Central authority is indifferent as to whether the starch requirement of the population is met by bread or potatoes.

Preoccupation with the ideological content has, until recently, tended to obscure the countless items toward which the Party attitude has always been essentially neutral. With economic improvement, many of the earlier practical objections to greater variety, better styling, and better marketing are disappearing. Thus there now exists a significant area of consumption where the conflict of wills between Central authority and the consumers is far less than may be supposed. There is today, in other words, a relatively wide area of consumption in respect to which Soviet authority has no reason, practical or ideological, for wishing to pursue any other policy than that of the maximization of consumer utility in its Western sense.

With the general improvement in the Soviet living standard, and thus in the expectations and capriciousness of the Soviet consumer, a twofold problem has emerged in this area of Party neutrality. (1) In the absence of the traditional market mechanism, how is one to know precisely what the consumers really prefer and when or in what direction their tastes are likely to shift? (2) Assuming such knowledge, what can be done to assure that the enterprises produce the desired output mix, quality, style, etc.? These were problems that hardly pressed for solution during the Stalinist period when the people of the Soviet Union were forced to do with the barest essentials of life. The general solution, which constitutes an important part of the current Soviet economic reforms, appears to lie in the direction of decentralization, greater local and enterprise initiative, and flexibility in regard to the amount and character of output; as well as in making it more profitable for the enterprise to relate its production to use-value.

To what extent do the above developments constitute a solid basis for concluding that the Soviet consumer is emerging sovereign? More generally, what evidence would support the convergence theory in regard to consumer freedom? A measure of the current relative size of the area of Party neutrality in consumption and, more important, a sense of the direction of change are critical. The Soviet consumer may be said to be gaining real freedom of choice if progressively more items of consumption are losing their ideological and practical content. To take the extreme case: if the Party were to become neutral toward all items of consumption, and the two problems cited above were solved, then the Soviet consumer would, indeed, be sovereign. Realistically, since there are significant limits to such freedom even in the most highly market-oriented economies, any comparison must be relative. The case for convergence is weakened, however, if the area of Party neutrality remains limited and if the Soviet consumer is free to choose only among those alternatives that do not contravene Party dogma. It is possible, of course, that the first case could lead to the second and there are those who base their optimism on its probability. But so much depends on what one assumes about the force of Marxist-Leninist ideology in present-day Russia, a point on which there is anything but universal agreement

Any conclusion about convergence should rest on many more factors and considerations than it has been possible to cover in this chapter. There is the matter, for instance, of the May, 1957, decentralization and the post-Khrushchev recentralization of the administrative structure of Soviet industry. Has the net effect of these changes on convergence been positive, negative, or, as might be suspected, neutral?

Assuming that the industrial reforms constitute a move toward a market orientation, is the same necessarily true in the case of the recent Soviet agricultural reforms? Are the latter reforms transforming the structure of Soviet agriculture from its dominantly collective (*kolkhoz*) form to some other? If so, is the change in the direction of free enterprise farming (an expansion of the private plot, peasant market system, for instance) or toward state (*sovkhoz*) farms?

Turning to a different aspect of this question, there are certain Soviet economists, Yevsei Liberman for instance, whose interests and suggested reforms center on the narrower problems of enterprise and consumer behavior. There are others, like L. S. Kantorovich, V. V. Novozhilov, or V. S. Memchinev, whose focus and work go far beyond Libermanism. They and their disciples have long been of the mind that the basic or central problems of any economy (rationality in regard to resource allocation, the price system, investment criteria, etc.) can finally be solved within the framework of a command economy. The search for a solution in the case of these economists lies in the use and further development of such techniques and concepts as mathematical economics, input-output, linear programming, and, most recently, with still further development of high-speed computers. It should be apparent, therefore, that any conclusion reached regarding the ultimate success or failure of centralized planning is closely linked with what one assumes about the realistic possibilities of these tools of economics and planning.

There remains the most general consideration of all: no economic system, whether capitalist or socialist, has ever existed in its "ideal" form. Thus the Soviet economy has all along contained elements of the market and the American elements of planning. This being so, the issue of convergence becomes fully meaningful only if some reasonable answer is offered to the following question: what is the essential difference between the Soviet and American economies as each exists in reality? It is not enough to point to differences in degree or cite the extent to which one relies on the market and the other on the planning principle. I am in full accord with Gregory Grossman when he writes, "There are many criteria for distinguishing between 'economic systems' and the undogmatic will refuse to be committed to any one of them."[12] The selection of some one criterion, however, must be tied to the purpose at hand; it must have operational significance. My focus differs from that of Grossman, therefore, in that it is more closely linked to the subject of this particular book.

Given our purpose, then, the basic distinction between the Soviet and American economies can most usefully be conceived of in terms of the *factors causing each to deviate from its theoretical ideal.* The American economy is fundamentally market oriented. There is a clear presumption here in favor of private ownership of the means of production and that framework which permits economic activity to be guided or determined by market forces. But few, even among the most ardent supporters of free enterprise, would question the necessity and desirability of placing elementary education, the military function, or interstate road construction within the public sector. Most would agree that public utilities should be subject to government controls. Serious debate begins in regard to what else, given this presumption in favor of a market economy, should or must be regulated or made part of the public sector.

Consider the same point from a somewhat different angle. Unhampered and uncontrolled, a market economy has been known to generate certain economic consequences which have been deemed by many to be socially, morally, or even aesthetically undesirable. A democratic government has numerous instruments—taxation, to mention but one—with which to alter the income, investment, consumption, or allocative pattern resulting from the free play of market forces. Direct governmental prohibition of the production and sale of narcotics for nonmedical purposes is commonly accepted as a desirable departure from the market ideal. Another, if less obvious, deviation is the taxation of spirits where the intent to curb consumption is more the point than the revenue objective. Again, the critical area of controversy is how much further the government ought to go in altering the market-determined pattern of income, investment, and consumption or the underlying pattern of resource allocation. To what degree, for example, should the progressive income tax be used as a means of income redistribution? In the face of recent medical evidence, should the government prohibit the manufacture and sale of tobacco as it does narcotics?

The Soviet economy, on the other hand, is planning or command oriented. In this case there is an equally clear presumption in favor of social ownership of the means of production and state control (centralized planning) of all economic activity. Here as well there are certain, though different, considerations which have compelled the Russians to depart from the planning ideal. Broadly speaking, these forces fall into one of two basic categories: those related to the human factor and those of a purely technical character. An illustration of each should help to clarify the point. The Soviet rulers have never denied their decided preference for the state farm over the agricultural collective, and especially its private plot of land feature. The agricultural collective emerged and continues to exist in large measure as a concession in the face of peasant resistance to total socialization of agriculture. This is not to deny that the Soviet regime was able to use the *kolkhoz* system to economic advantage during the years of rapid industrialization, inasmuch as peasant income was a residual rather than a wage.

Turning to the second category, the planning ideal presumes a sophistication of planning theory and practice, or a level of omniscience on the part of Central authority, that simply does not exist. It requires an exactitude, an ability to coordinate infinite variables and strike delicate balances, for which, to take the most optimistic view, techniques have not yet been devised or perfected. As a consequence, random deviations from the planning ideal occur, and planners are sometimes forced to seek a market solution for a time at least.

Thus the word *presumption* turns out to be the strategic concept in arriving at a fundamental distinction between the two types of economies. An economy may be said to be basically capitalist or free enterprise where, by consensus, there exists a clear presumption in favor of private ownership of the means of production and the market principle. The burden of proof that it is necessary or desirable to depart from the ideal falls on those who advocate additional governmental controls or a further enlargement of the public sector. A socialist or command economy, by the same token, is one where the doctrinal presumption is just as clearly in favor of social ownership of the productive means and the planning principle. Here the burden of proof rests with those who see the necessity or advocate deviations from the planning ideal. Viewed in this way, therefore, modern economies may be classified as either market or planning oriented, with the word "system" best reserved to denote that particular mixture of the two basic elements which actually characterizes a given economy at a point in time. Thus it may be further possible to differentiate between, say, the Soviet economic system and the Yugoslavian economic system, even though both may be planning oriented.

This brings us to the last and broadest series of questions in regard to the current Soviet economic reforms. (1) Do these reforms represent a change in Soviet presumption, that is, a shift from a planning to a market orientation? (2) Or do these reforms constitute a deviation, if a more complex one than in the past, from the planning ideal? This implies, of course, that there is at least one important school of Soviet economists that is continuing to search for a solution to present-day Soviet economic problems that is consistent with the planning ideal. (3) How far can the Soviets deviate from the planning ideal, in the effort to cope with such economic problems, before this very deviation turns into a change in the presumption itself? It is in the answer to this third question that the evidence is the most elusive, the difference of opinion among specialists the greatest, and the case for or against convergence most easily made.

II

The Current Soviet Planning Reforms*

Abram Bergson

Recently announced decisions of the Soviet government to reform its planning system have been greeted in the West as a momentous international event. The changes being made are surely not quite as dramatic as this assumes, but the government is reorganizing, often in novel ways, its proverbially centralized arrangements for industrial planning, and it has good reason to do so.

Although some of the reforms are novel, one of

* To my profit, Gregory Grossman kindly commented on a preliminary draft. I have also benefited from discussions with other colleagues.

them, concerning the administrative structure of industry, is hardly so. Prior to May, 1957, branch ministries were preeminent in industry, but Khrushchev at that time supplanted this traditional apparatus with one in which regional authorities became primary. Khrushchev acted with much fanfare, but his successors apparently have concluded that the branch-ministerial form of organization is superior, and no doubt with some basis, though Khrushchev may not always have been so "hare-brained" as charged. In any event, the government has now decreed reestablishment of the branch ministries. As the latest example of the familiar Soviet proclivity for bureaucratic reshuffling, this reversal is not without interest, but Western attention has properly been directed to other changes being made in industrial planning that are relatively novel.

Of the reforms in question, the chief were initiated at a meeting of the Central Committee of the Communist Party held during September 27–29, 1965. As elaborated in a report submitted to the Central Committee by Premier Alexsei N. Kosygin,[1] and in the numerous, although not always revealing, decrees, instructions, and commentaries which (as is characteristic in the U.S.S.R.) followed immediately in the wake of the Central Committee action, the

September, 1965, program is more complex than many reports might suggest.

To refer only to bare essentials, the agency at the lowest bureaucratic level in Soviet industry, and hence the one immediately in charge of operations, is the *predpriiatie,* or enterprise. This has been so whether branch-ministerial or regional agencies have been preeminent, and will still be so now that the branch-ministerial system is again the order of the day. Under centralized planning, enterprise management has not been subject to control from above to quite the minute degree often supposed, but its authority has been severely limited. Under the new program, such authority is to be expanded. This will occur through a reduction in the number of the enterprise's plan targets that must be approved by superior agencies, and also in other ways. Thus, in utilizing available wage funds, enterprise management previously was much constrained by targets for wage payments, for employment, and for average earnings for different categories of workers. Now management will be subject to only one such target, for total wages paid to all workers. Within the limits of the total fund assigned it, the management may employ labor as it wishes. Scales of basic wage rates for different categories of workers, however, will continue to be determined primarily by superior agencies.[2]

Decisions on capital investments hitherto have been especially centralized, but through charges to profits and depreciation, each enterprise is now to establish a "fund for the growth of production," which it may use with some discretion to finance modernization, automation, and various other capital investment projects. Since, for industry generally, funds for the growth of production are expected to finance about 20 per cent of state capital investment in 1966, the additional authority gained at this point could be of some consequence.[3]

Enterprise management is also to be allowed greater discretion in some other, related ways. Thus, it may now decide whether and to what extent piece (rather than time) work is to be employed in determining wages; it has more authority than before in respect to custom production, and so on.

Plan targets in the U.S.S.R. constitute at once standards of performance, "success criteria," for enterprise management, but necessarily not all targets can have equal weight. Interestingly, then, not only are targets approved by superior agencies being reduced in number; to some extent they are also being changed in character, and apparently also in their relative importance. Among other things, targets for output, including unfinished goods and stocks, which were previously stressed, are to give way to one for "realized production," or sales.[4] Contrary to many reports, profits have long been calculated in the U.S.S.R. but now the target for profits is also to become an important test of performance.

Along with success criteria, changes are also being made in arrangements for managerial bonuses. These affect managerial behavior under Soviet socialism hardly less than elsewhere. Thus, bonuses, which hitherto have been based chiefly on performance relative to the plan target for output, are henceforth to depend primarily on performance relative to plan targets for sales and profits. Bonuses are to vary according to the degree of fulfillment of one of these two targets, but will be conditional on fulfillment of the other. The bonuses will also be conditional on satisfactory performance regarding other matters, such as the assortment of goods produced.

Then, too, such managerial bonuses, together with some premia for workers generally, are now to be paid out of a new "fund for material encouragement," which is to be maintained to a considerable extent through charges from profits. The charges are to vary according to an intricate system that is not easily summarized and that perhaps will not always be readily grasped by managerial personnel themselves. Suffice it to say that appropriations will depend not only on sales and profits, but on other indicators of performance, including "profitability," a Soviet euphemism for the rate of return on capital. Regarding sales and profits, what will count is performance relative not only to the plan but to pre-plan levels. The government is also establishing new arrangements for rewarding the introduction of new products, and hopes to heighten interest in satisfactory performance generally through diverse changes in procedures for financing of housing, nurseries, and the like, that are administered by the enterprise.[5]

Last but not least, the changes in success criteria are to be accompanied by revisions in financial and price-fixing practices.[6] According to a strange but long-standing policy, new capital hitherto has been made available to enterprises for the most part in the form of interest-free grants from the government budget. In future, however, enterprises will have to pay a charge out of their profits on their capital (typically 6 per cent). The enterprises will also have to finance their capital needs increasingly through repayable loans. A firm which enjoys an especially favorable position regarding natural resources may also be subjected to a fixed "rental" payment.

For the rest, the manner in which price-fixing practices will be changed is still under study. Apparently, industrial wholesale prices, which usually are fixed to allow a standard mark-up over average branch cost, but which for the most part have not been changed since July 1, 1955, are at long last to be updated. In the process, the prices presumably will also be altered to allow for the novel charges on capital and rental payments.

In advancing the new program, Kosygin was careful to explain that it will be implemented only in the course of time. Although the government has clearly committed itself to the reform, it apparently expects to review it as it is being put into practice. In fact, the new arrangements affecting enterprise autonomy, success criteria, and finance began to be introduced only in January, 1966, and at that time only for forty-three enterprises. In April, 1966, however, the new arrangements were extended to an additional two hundred enterprises, and Kosygin explained in his report to the twenty-third Party Congress that by the beginning of 1967 enterprises operating under the new reforms will employ one-third of all industrial workers.[7] The reform in industrial prices, declaredly, is to be carried out in 1967 and 1968.

I have been referring to the reform program initiated by Kosygin at the Party Central Committee meeting of September, 1965. Prior to the Central Committee meeting, the government had already experimentally initiated changes in planning for consumer goods industries much like the changes now being instituted in industry generally. The experimental changes were first introduced in two clothing firms, the Bol'shevichka and Maiak, in the summer of 1964, and then, in 1965, were extended to several hundred enterprises producing clothing, shoes, leather, and textiles. Under this earlier experiment, procedures different from those being introduced under the September, 1965, program were sometimes employed. Among other things, the enterprises affected were given much discretion to determine the assortment of goods produced in response to orders received from wholesale and retail trade outlets. Often such enterprises also gained more authority in other spheres than is now being given industrial enterprises generally under Kosygin's later reform. Procedures employed under the experiment, however, varied in the course of time and between enterprises, and are in any event often difficult to judge from the incomplete information available. The experiment remains of interest because the government intends to continue it in operation, and probably will further broaden its scope while it reorganizes industry generally in accord with the reforms projected by Kosygin in September, 1965.[8]

In sum, the Soviet government is scarcely dismantling wholesale its system of centralized industrial planning, as sometimes has been suggested in the West, but it is adapting this system measurably in the direction of decentralization and increased use of market-type controls.[9] The adaptation, moreover, cannot be very palatable to a political group which has been bred ideologically to view market institutions as a source of anarchy, and is sensitive to the threat to their authoritarian rule and the bureaucratic status of superior personnel that is inherent in any consequential economic shifts in the direction now taken. Why is the government at long last initiating such changes?

The U.S.S.R., it has been reported,[10] is "going through a crisis as profound, if not as eye-catching, as capitalism's crisis in the 1930's." This is hardly accurate, but the government is manifestly concerned about the onerous responsibilities which superior agencies in the bureaucratic structure must bear under centralized planning. Subject to approval at the highest level, such agencies must, among other things, determine in essentials the volume and direction of capital investment. They also have major responsibilities for the coordination of myriads of plan targets, and for the control of current factor inputs, especially of materials, fuel, power, and machinery that are required to implement the plan.

With such responsibilities the superior agencies

understandably find it difficult to cope, and one must read partly in this light complaints that lately have become commonplace even in the U.S.S.R. such as this: "The basic flaw in planning and management was that every detail was supposed to be decided from the center and, since it was impossible to know the circumstances at each enterprise, the center proceeded from average conditions that did not exist in reality in any one enterprise, and added an approximate average rate of growth, which was low for some and intolerable for other enterprises." [11]

Or this: "There are also irregularities in deliveries and incomplete deliveries; the grades, types and sizes of materials ordered are frequently replaced by other less economic ones. For example, the Ukraine Chief Supply and Marketing Administration sent the Novo-Kakhova Electrical Machinery Plant a large amount of 750 x 1,500 mm. sheet steel for dynamos instead of 860 x 1,720 mm. sheet; as a result the coefficient of use of the metal dropped by 23 per cent.

"Shortcomings in supply also affect the economics of enterprises. . . . At the Rostov Farm Machinery Plant, for example, there were approximately 11,000 substitutions of rolled metal shapes and dimensions in five years—that is, an average of seven substitutions a day; this resulted in an overexpenditure of more than 22,000 tons of metal. Frequently there are also huge losses from the low quality of products supplied, in particular cast parts." [12]

Or this: "Because of the absence of equipment, there are now about 1.5 million square meters of deserted productive floor space. In the textile department of the Kursk Synthetic Fiber Kombinat more than 3,000 square meters of floor space have been empty since 1960. In the 'Tadzhiktekstilmash' Factory around 5,000 square meters of productive floor space . . . have been idle for more than two years because of the lack of specialized equipment." [13]

The government understandably is now seeking to lighten responsibilities of superior agencies. Since managers of enterprises have often complained of the "petty tutelage" to which they are subject, it is also hoped that the authority transferred to them will be exercised more effectively than it was by their superiors.

The government has no less reason to reform managerial success criteria, however, for within their limited sphere enterprise managers also act wastefully, and curiously they are even impelled to do so by the success criteria that have prevailed.[14] Even with a "visible hand" replacing an "invisible" one, as it has turned out, what is good for the individual enterprise is by no means always good for the country.

Thus, the infamous "safety factor" which is also a

familiar theme in the U.S.S.R.: enterprise managers of necessity are allowed to negotiate with superior agencies regarding their plan targets, and in doing so seek to limit their assignments. In this way they hope more easily to earn bonuses for plan fulfillment. To the same end, the managers also hesitate to overfulfill targets, for fear that subsequent goals will only be made higher.

In trying especially to fulfill the target for gross output, managers also often find it possible, and even expedient, to stress inordinately goods that bulk large physically. Alternatively, where gross output is calculated in value terms emphasis may be placed on products that have relatively high ruble prices, but such prices also have their limitations, so the resulting assortment again may be strange. Thus the unending reports of difficulties of the Soviet consumer in shopping for particular items: for example, in buying large-size boys' shoes, as distinct from small-size men's shoes; of shirt, as distinct from bandage, cloth; of small-size as distinct from large-size electric bulbs, and so on.

Almost inevitably shortcuts are also taken regarding quality: as in the Russian Soviet Federated Socialist Republic, where among products examined by inspectors of the Ministry of Trade in the first half of 1962, 32.7 per cent of the clothing articles, 25 per cent of the knitwear, and 32.6 per cent of the leather shoes were rejected or reclassified in a lower quality category; or in the Ukraine, where 20 to 25 per cent of the clothing and knitwear examined by the Ministry of Trade during 1963 had to be condemned as defective; or where a factory manufacturing tractor parts found it advantageous to overfulfill its output goal by 60 per cent while lowering the quality of its products and so reducing their useful life by 40 to 50 per cent. In order to fulfill the current target for output, managers also hesitate to introduce new products, and find it profitable to abuse their machinery. The list of managerial aberrations could easily be lengthened still further.

In the determination of wholesale prices for industrial goods, the rule has long been simply to cover average branch cost.[15] Whereas a modest planned profit is also allowed, no charge has been included in cost for interest on fixed capital or rent for scarce resources. The rule nevertheless has often been honored in the breach, and sometimes the prices must be closer to scarcity values than they otherwise would be, but often too, they must have been even less so. Most importantly, as noted, prices generally have been left unchanged since the last major price reform of July, 1955. For this reason alone, prices must frequently differ far from costs as well as scarcity values generally.

As determined in these ways, ruble prices evidently bear the earmarks of obsolete doctrine, particularly the Marxian labor theory of value, as well as of cumbersome central planning. But the effect on the relation of prices to scarcity values is much the same in either case, and curiously the very divergencies from such values is itself a major reason why the task of superior agencies is so difficult. For such agencies to calculate in terms of such prices is not easy, but it is no easier for them to calculate otherwise. As indicated, the dubious prices have also been a source of distortion in the behavior of enterprise management and they only promise to become more so as far as sales and profits are to be cardinal success criteria. Regarding prices, too, therefore, there is both room and need for improvement, though the government has yet to commit itself on the precise changes that will be made. It is also seeking to make success criteria more valid by revising procedures for financing of capital investment.

These deficiencies in centralized planning are hardly new; they had already become manifest in the early Five-Year Plans under Stalin. Why is the government only now taking any consequential action to alleviate them? Reform might have been in order long ago, but it has become especially so lately because of the ever increasing complexity of the task with which the cumbersome system of industrial planning must grapple. In Western comment on the current Soviet economic scene, this trend is properly often referred to. The task is becoming more complex because of the continually growing number of industrial enterprises (recently 200,000 of "census" size [16]), whose interrelationships must be planned; because of the ever increasing variety of commodities that such plants supply (according to a "complete" classification, an estimated 20 million items are now in production [17]); and because of the ever more exacting requirements of modern technology.

The complexity is also greater because the government's own aim is no longer simply to produce steel and then more steel, as it was under Stalin. In his famous attack on Gosplan men in "steel blinkers," Khrushchev, of course, meant to urge not merely a greater use of plastics, but a more flexible outlook on alternative industrial branches generally. Despite their criticism of Khrushchev, his successors probably will hesitate to abandon altogether this particular policy.[18] Moreover, the government, which in the face of crop shortages has been importing about 20 million tons of grain since mid-1963, is also more attentive to consumers than it was under Stalin. For the dictator, food shortages did not even preclude exports. And the task of directing economic activity has become the more intricate because, though still not affluent, the consumers themselves have become more choosy, as witness the quite new phenomenon in the U.S.S.R. of overstocks of consumer goods of less desirable sizes and styles.[19]

If prevailing priorities reflect a greater awareness of alternatives, this must be owing partly to another development which has also been favorable to economic reform in other ways as well. The pretensions of poor Comrade Yaroshenko to the contrary notwithstanding, Stalin had held that "the directing bodies" must reserve for themselves consideration of the "rational organization of the productive forces, economic planning, etc." Hence, these vital topics could not be the subject matter of a "political economy of socialism" open to inquiry by economists generally.[20] Yet the government has now found it expedient to allow economists generally to explore these very same questions. In doing so, the economists are even permitted to use forms of analysis, especially of a mathematical sort, formerly regarded as *bourgeois*, and so taboo.

The invigorated economics that has quickly

emerged has itself been a factor in the equation indicating economic reform. Thus, much of the Soviet criticism of planning procedures that has been referred to is to be found in the writings of Soviet economists themselves. The reforms now being implemented, it has been reported, were largely shaped by the ideas of the Kharkov economist, Yevsei Liberman. In fact, many other Soviet economists have also contributed, but the U.S.S.R. too now has its influential "new economics," and the new reforms bear its stamp.[21]

Scarcely less momentous than these developments, however, has been another: as reported, the rate of economic growth has declined, and markedly, according to both official Soviet and Western calculations, though the former as usual seem inflated:

Real national income, average annual % increase [22]

	SOVIET OFFICIAL DATA	WESTERN DATA
1950–1958	10.9	7.0
1958–1959	7.5	4.2
1959–1960	7.7	4.9
1960–1961	6.8	6.8
1961–1962	5.7	4.3
1962–1963	4.1	2.6
1963–1964	9.0	7.2
1964–1965	6.	3.

Even the reduced rates are still respectable, but the decline must be disconcerting for proponents of a social system whose asserted economic superiority is held to be observable, above all, in its ability to generate rapid growth. And, still worse, the rival capitalist system in the West lately has itself shown unexpected capabilities in this regard, first in Western Europe and most recently even in the United States. To "overtake and surpass" the advanced capitalist countries economically can no longer seem the easy task that the ebullient Khrushchev assumed not so long ago.

By all accounts, economic growth has declined in the U.S.S.R. for diverse reasons, and among these some of the most important, such as those causing the continued stagnation in agriculture,[23] are remote from deficiencies in industrial planning. By repairing these deficiencies, however, the government hopes to assure an increasingly effective use of productive factors in industry, and on this basis to offset more successfully retarding forces affecting the economy generally.

As Kosygin made clear in his September, 1965, report, the government seeks increased effectiveness in the use of all productive factors, but especially capital. Even when growth was rapid, it could be achieved only by a disproportionately rapid increase in the capital stock. Now that growth has slowed, the increase in capital stock has become inordinate. To continue to rely so heavily on capital inputs as a source of growth necessarily would mean that the share of total output going to current capital investment, which already may be one-third, must rise still higher. Only in this way could the government hope to find the wherewithal to assure a continuing increase in the capital stock more rapid than the increase in output.[24] By implication, supplies of goods available to provide long-promised gains for consumers would likely be meager. Through improved planning procedures the government seeks to arrest the rise in capital coefficient which currently besets it, and so to limit the increases in the investment rate and encroachments on consumption that will be needed for future growth.

In reporting to the Party Central Committee in September, 1965, Kosygin expressed confidence that "with tireless work" the measures being undertaken would yield "beneficial results."[25] Although he referred primarily to the reforms that he had proposed to the Central Committee, the government obviously is of the same view regarding the rearrangement that already had been made experimentally for consumer goods enterprises. How beneficial will the results be?

Under the reforms, the responsibilities of superior agencies will be somewhat diminished, but will still be onerous. Still, the experiment in consumer goods industries has, as reported, brought a marked improvement in quality and assortment in many enterprises, but this has often been achieved in the face of adverse profit margins which could be discouraging under other than experimental conditions. Difficulties have also been encountered in procuring through the still cumbersome supply system materials needed for an improved assortment. Under the September, 1965, reforms, appropriations to the enterprise's bonus fund are to depend partly on the projected improvement in its performance over the previous year, and the government hopes on this basis to weaken the "safety factor." Perhaps it will, but it remains to be seen to what extent, under the intricate incentive procedures being established, management will be interested in foregoing use of this device. Successes in this regard have been reported among the forty-three enterprises placed under the reforms in January, 1964, though one wonders again how typical such initial experiences will prove to be.

Under both the experiment in consumer goods industries and the September, 1965, reforms, the government also has reason to expect managerial performance to improve in other spheres, but here, too, difficulties have arisen which may prove more than episodic: a wholesale oil supply base seeking to fulfill its target for sales compelled its customers, by the threat of fines, to fulfill their contracts, though as a result of operating economies the customers' requirements had declined; management's newly won discretion as to investment has been balked by difficulties in obtaining needed services of construction agencies; the enterprise autonomy generally is still constrained by red tape and improper encroachments of superior agencies.[26]

When adversities have been encountered, the still dubious prices are sometimes a factor, and the projected reform in such prices should be to the good. But the principles to be observed in fixing the new prices are not yet settled, and even after such prices prevail, the bureaucratic reluctance to change them will still be deleterious.

In sum, time alone can tell what will be achieved, but even a proponent of Western market institutions may feel that resort to such arrangements in such a limited fashion in a strange environment is apt to yield only limited gains. By implication, the government may soon find the system of industrial planning again on its agenda, though in changed circumstances. Possibly it will refrain from further reforms but this would not be promising, and it would be no more so to abandon the reforms now in progress, though this, too, is possible.

The government is now promoting the use of mathematical economics and advanced computers, and some enthusiastic proponents of these tools have held that they will permit centralized planning to work after all, so that decentralization and market-type controls can be obviated. But the government thus far has properly been guided by a more responsible view that mathematical analysis and computers can be helpful, but are hardly a solution to the problem of planning organization. In a complex modern economy, with myriads of unknowns to be determined, perfect computation is conceptually intriguing as the electronic analogue of the perfect competition of economic theory, but scarcely a practicality.[27]

The government is not about to restore capitalism, and Soviet economists have rightly criticized commentators, both in China and the West, who have suggested as much, but it may not be easy to confine the market to limits now being observed. Another characterization of the current reforms also suggested, therefore, may not really be amiss: "creeping capitalism." It will be fascinating to see how in the years ahead the government grapples with its complex problem of planning organization.

III

The Politics of Soviet Economic Reform

John N. Hazard

Economic policy is closely associated with political consequences in the minds of Soviet leaders. This has been so since the Revolution, when Lenin found it possible to say, "Do not separate administration from politics."[1] His theme has been repeated by each leader of the U.S.S.R. in the nearly fifty years that have elapsed since the October Revolution. Administrative reform may seem to be a bewildering mass of technical details capable of exciting interest only among specialists in economics and public administration, but there is always a strong political motivation in the U.S.S.R. A 1946 textbook reminded its readers, "The basic task of the organs of Soviet socialist administration, just as is the case with all other organs of the Soviet state, is the construction of communist society." [2] Premier Alexsei N. Kosygin is only the most recent to restate the axiom in introducing the reforms of 1965. He reminded his listeners, "The correct solution of these questions has enormous political and practical significance." [3]

Political consequences in the Soviet context have usually been discerned on two levels: that of broad social trends affecting institutional relationships generally, and that concerning the ambitions of a single man. Some explained Nikita Khrushchev's decentralization of 1957 as the latter when he abolished economic ministries and created regional economic councils. This move was interpreted as a clever means of clearing Moscow of potential personal enemies by sending the industrial ministers to the provinces. Others took it for what Khrushchev said it was: a move designed to improve efficiency in fulfillment of his thesis that the "chief thing in the building of communism is economics, production, the struggle to create material and spiritual benefits for man." [4]

The tracing of personal motivation and intrigue in administrative reform is a fascinating pursuit, but it is only for those who have inside information on personal motivation either from association with Communist leaders or from minute examination of biographies over long periods of time. Without such insight my observation must be limited to what may be determined from evident broad social trends and institutional relationships. From these there can be noted the emergence since Lenin's time of three crucial relationships. It is to an examination of the potential impact of the 1965 administrative reforms on these relationships that this chapter is devoted. They are: (1) the role played by the Communist Party with respect to state institutions; (2) the role played by the republics in relationship to the federal government; and (3) the emergence, with ever increasing industrialization, of potentially influential interest groups.

The administrative reforms of 1965 were preceded a year earlier by the ouster of Khrushchev and a fundamental reform of the structure of the Communist Party. Khrushchev had innovated beyond all expectation in 1962 [5] when he persuaded the Central Committee of the Party to bring Party cadres closer to economic operation, if not to put them directly into the administrative process previously reserved for the officials of the state mechanism. This he had done by inspiring a splitting of the cadres into two groups, those specializing in agricultural production and those specializing in industry. This was a reversal of the long-standing policy of utilizing the Party members as leaders, not as operators, as generalists rather than specialists.

Lenin had kept the apparatus of the Party and that of the state separate ever since he called upon the institutions of the "soviets" to become the state apparatus for the new Russia. So did Stalin, until the crisis of the Second World War when he concerned himself directly with state operations; but even with his personal assumption as General Secretary of the Party of the position of Chairman of the Council of People's Commissars, he proclaimed the continuing importance for operating purposes of the state's civil servants. His Party cadres came closer to operations than at any previous time in Soviet history, but they were cautioned always to remain sufficiently aloof to give them time to think of the fundamental problems and to avoid becoming enmeshed in detail.

Khrushchev's henchmen tried to preserve Lenin's principle, at least in words, for an *Izvestia* columnist wrote in December, 1962, "It must be profoundly understood that the Party is taking a decisive turn toward production. . . . But, the Party is not the commander, but the ideological and political leader of the people." [6]

The words of caution proved to be only words, for

the Party cadres increased in number to perform their duties as supervisors of detail. A *Pravda* editorial later complained, "Instead of simplifying and lowering the cost of production in the past two years, the [Party] apparatus of province and territory has grown substantially."[7] The Party rolls expanded swiftly to push the total up nearly one-fifth in two years.[8] Clearly, Khrushchev's policy had driven the Party cadres into paper work as politically oriented clerks and had minimized their role as thinkers, as ideologists. Some outsiders reported after prolonged visits to the U.S.S.R. that Party membership had lost its militant leadership feature and was being granted, like British knighthoods or Empire Medals, to persons doing significant things. Even a non-Party astronaut while circling the globe radioed back his desire to become a Party member and Khrushchev granted it on the spot from his telephone.

Khrushchev's transformation of the Party into a corps of politically oriented administrators was probably a major reason for his ouster in October, 1964. Proof of this conclusion lies in the almost immediate reversal of what he had done two years earlier. On November 16, 1964,[9] the Central Committee of the Party put an end to the division into agricultural and industrial sectors. It restored the system established by Lenin and built upon by Stalin, under which the

Party became again a unity, a master of all subjects, a corps of men and women trained in techniques of production but serving primarily as generalists, as jacks of all trades.

The Party's journal of practice, *Partinaia Zhizn,* explained the motives for the reversal by saying, "Today the executive posts at enterprises, collective farms, state farms, institutions, and organizations are on the whole filled by experienced, qualified individuals who are capable of analyzing the concrete problems of production and of educating people. . . . They do not need irksome reminders and pressures which create an atmosphere of nervousness and lack of confidence in one's abilities or the imposition of stereotyped directions without regard for local experience. Such a practice—and, unfortunately, it still exists in some places—runs counter to the Party's instructions and contradicts the Leninist style in Party and economic guidance." [10]

The wording of the Central Committee's resolution of November 16 put the issue bluntly by saying, "For the purpose of strengthening the guiding role of the Party and its local bodies in communist construction . . . it is necessary to return to the principle of structuring Party organizations on a territorial-production basis." This meant going back to the old forms under which the Party had no functional sectors responsible for details in the administration of agriculture or industry.

Symbols of the reversal of Khrushchev's policy were provided at the very top of the Party-state structure. Roles which he had combined in his own person in 1957 as First Secretary of the Party and as Chairman of the Council of Ministers were separated, as they had been throughout most of the history of the U.S.S.R., and Leonid Brezhnev and Kosygin took up their respective posts as leaders of two separate services. Although some foreign interpreters have seen the move as reflecting the inability of either man to seize total power, the change seems more likely to have been dictated by sound organizational principles. Nowhere, whether inside the U.S.S.R. or beyond its borders, whether in government or in private enterprise, is strength gained by placing both the idea-giving and the administrative functions in one man's hands when the enterprise to be administered becomes gigantic. Clearly, the Party leaders who ousted Khrushchev thought their collective strength enhanced by what they had done, and foreign analysts can be read to agree with them.

Thus, Leonard Schapiro of the University of London, who has gained wide reputation as an astute analyst of the ebb and flow of Party power in the U.S.S.R., saw Khrushchev's policy as a debilitating factor for the leadership function of the Party. Speaking of the role of the Party secretary at the regional (*oblast*) level under the system of split cadres specializing in agricultural and industrial production, he noted, "The regional first secretary, in the case of a functionally divided region, is no longer party boss of a whole region, but only of one branch of economic life within the region. His authority has also been reduced as a result of the fact that his diocese no longer corresponds to the much enlarged area of the new Councils of National Economy. . . . As for the party committee secretary [for agriculture] again he is no longer the sole party overlord within his own boundaries: he has been incorporated in an elaborate technical agricultural organization. . . ."[11]

An American analyst has referred to the Khrushchev period of intimate merger between Party and state apparatus as giving rise to questions as to why the Party continued to exist at all, and has concluded that the 1964 reversal has caused the Party to reemerge as a distinct structure within the Soviet political system.[12]

Judging from some experience in public administration in the United States, I must agree with those who see the 1964 restructuring of the Party as an effort to regain Party initiative. The leaders' intention is to recreate a corps of generalists thinking and synthesizing experience. This elite is to look beyond immediate problems of daily and yearly plan fulfillment to the course of Soviet socialism generally. Perhaps this accounts for the professed wish to retard the growth of the Party, to which reference has already been made. No longer is nearly every top administrator to be invited to join Party ranks. The Party will return in some measure to the narrow elite of thinkers and political organizers which Lenin envisioned when he laid the base in 1905.

The return to Leninism was dramatically demonstrated in revisions in Party rules proposed at the Twenty-third Congress in 1966.[13] Admission is to be made more difficult by requiring that letters of recommendation come from members of five years' standing rather than three. Discipline is to be strengthened by restoring to the Party rules the penalty of expulsion for violation of rules, and the penalty is to be exacted more frequently than in the Khrushchev period. Demotion to the status of candidate is not to be accepted as a substitute for expulsion.

Whether the Party can succeed in regaining its lost prestige no one can say. There are voices outside the U.S.S.R. who think that the time has passed for a Party which limits its numbers and makes no claim to movement toward a society where the public generally can share through multi-candidate elections in the selection of men and women to make policy in its name.[14] The proceedings of the Twenty-third Party Congress seem to suggest that leaders see the danger of Khrushchev's road away from the elite concept. Party control is being strengthened over elements in society who utilize opportunities created for them by expanded freedom to express competing ideas.

Kosygin found it desirable, in announcing the return to the ministerial system of industrial administration, to say that he was not returning to the pre-Khrushchev pattern. In abolishing Khrushchev's economic regional administrative boards, the Party was planning to avoid Stalin's extreme centralization, which had evolved after 1923 with a decrease in the administrative responsibilities of the various republics making up the union The reform of 1965 called for a combination of the features familiar to a ministerial system based on administration of branches of the economy in "the integral development of the national economy as a whole," but with more emphasis on "the economies of the country's republics and regions, with expansion of the economic powers of the republics." [15]

Kosygin's emphasis upon the economic role of the republics was put into practice by two institutional changes in Stalin's system. Several of the key branches of industry are not to be organized on the all-union structure of Stalin's time, when orders from Moscow directed all operations of the plants in the field. The pattern to be used under the 1965 reform is that of the union-republic ministry, conceived originally in 1923 to combine centralized planning with local operations, but never used by key branches of the economy. Thus, industries engaged in steel, nonferrous metals, coal, chemicals, and petroleum drilling and refining [16] pass, under Kosygin's plan, to the combined attention of both center and republics, each sharing in their administration as was possible only in the consumer goods industries under Stalin.

Even those few key construction industries restored to the all-union type of industrial ministry are to be denied the independence of local authority granted them by Stalin. The republics are to share in the planning of their programs, for "The Republic State Planning Committees are also to develop proposals for draft production plans for enterprises that are situated in the republics but are under all-union jurisdiction." [17]

It is these features which permit Kosygin to conclude, "At first glance it may seem that a simple return to the former ministries is being proposed. But to think this means to ignore the new circumstances, is to make a mistake. The ministries that are being organized will work in wholly different conditions. . . ."[18]

To grasp the nature of the revised status of republics, one must note the place of this unit in the Soviet system of government. The republics are not to be compared in origin to the states of the United States, for they were created on the basis of ethnic groups. Their boundaries correspond to ethnic rather than economic factors. The ethnic component was necessary to gain the adherence of suspicious minorities reluctant to return to a state system in which the Russians had traditionally dominated the Tsarist unitary state.

The compelling importance of the political reason for federation was emphasized in 1927 when the State Planning Commission was authorized to redraw the boundaries of provinces in the U.S.S.R. to conform to economic reality.[19] When planners asked whether ethnic boundaries were to take precedence over those economically justifiable, the answer came back from the highest Party body that this precedence was to be preserved. This policy remained in effect until 1956, when a first breach was made by termination of the Karelo-Finnish Republic's status as a union-republic with its reincorporation into the Russian Republic, on the ground that its economy was a unity with that of the Russians.[20] Later the explanation was given that the Finns had become an inconsequential factor in this expanding industrial area, and there was no reason to preserve frontiers based on ethnic grounds alone.

A second step in giving precedence to economics appeared in 1962 in central Asia when the economies of five republics were brought together under the direction of a Central Asian Regional Economic Council.[21]

Hints as to the direction being followed by Khrushchev came from a Soviet speaker at the Stockholm conference of the International Political Science Association of 1962, when he noted that the role of the republics was being rethought in preparation for a new constitution. Speculation was rife, even among Soviet scholars, that there would be a merger of the two chambers of the Supreme Soviet to reduce, if not eliminate, the representation by republic.

All of this began to change with Khrushchev's ouster. Professor A. I. Lepeshkin, as the Academy of Science's expert on public law, called for restudy of the relationship between the center and the republics, "especially now, when the experiment in setting up individual major economic regions and forming inter-republic economic bodies within them has failed to justify itself." [22]

The Central Asian Regional Economic Council was dissolved,[23] and a Soviet professor speaking at a Strasbourg seminar in April, 1966, found it possible to predict that even if the ethnic reason for federation were to be weakened as all peoples of the U.S.S.R. developed economically to a point where no one feared domination by the major ethnic group, a federal structure might well be retained because of the advantages of decentralization of state administration.

What he was saying has some meaning in light of the fact that not only has the population of the former Karelo-Finnish Republic become an amalgam of many peoples employed in the expanding industry of the region, but in the Kazakh Republic of central Asia, the peoples from which the republic gained its name are now in the minority. There has been a great influx of others of quite different racial stock to man the industries built during and since the war.

The conclusion is compelling that either republics are actually regaining the authority that was being drained away under Khrushchev, or they are being encouraged to think that such authority is being regained. More important, this resurrection of local authority is occurring for reasons not present in 1923; it is not for need of pacifying a renascent nationalism, although there have been some manifestations of ethnic pride in vocal elements of the population, but because of the expectation that economic efficiency can be enhanced through a system which shares decision-making between central planners and regional administrators.

Kosygin distinguished his economic reform from Stalin's method of administration not only because of a new attitude toward the authority of the republics but because of "expanded economic independence of enterprises." [24] Economists have detailed the nature of these powers, but the political consequence in strengthening the role of industrial managers requires exploration. Kosygin left no doubt that a strengthened enterprise means a strengthened director. He noted, "The cadres of industrial managers bear full personal responsibility for the sector of production entrusted to them by the state. This responsibility, the role of one-man management in production, is growing especially now." To the outsider there emerges the prospect of an industrial tsar.

There is nothing new in the idea, for Lenin called for such individual responsibility of managers as early as December, 1918, in condemning the lack of responsibility inherent in the committee system introduced into Russian factories after the Revolution. He thought the committees simply inefficient, since no one is responsible when all are responsible. To remedy this situation, he proposed that each member of the committee be given a specific task and be made to account for his performance.[25]

The one-man goal was restated by the Ninth Communist Party Congress of March, 1920,[26] and was made the rule at the Fourteenth Congress of 1925.[27] Still, change came slowly, for reasons explained by Stalin in 1931 as "[there are] not enough persons who are familiar with the questions of technique, economics and finance." [28] To remedy this inadequacy, the Party's Central Committee in 1929 ordered managers to learn all processes of production, not limiting themselves to general questions of administration; and to strengthen the managers' hands, the Party ordered trade unions not to interfere directly in administration. It even told the Communist Party cell in each factory, "The administration must not be subordinated to the party cell." [29]

From that moment appeared the specter of a potentially independent, and hence politically powerful, interest group devoid of direct control by trade union and Party, but the managers were individuals working without organization. There was no institution through which to focus their power on policy making, no National Association of Industrial Managers. They were recognized only as a shadowy force, lacking much influence because both the trade union and local Party officials refused to accept the restrictions laid down in 1929 and insisted on participation in managerial decisions in what came to be known as a three-way administrative board, the "triangle."

Threat of war changed the picture, and Stalin, in perceiving the need for mobilization, took swift action. Without warning, in 1927 he ordered the "triangle" body never to meet again because the trade union and Party members were hampering efficiency and independent decision-making by managers. Directors surged forward and became a powerful element of each community during the war. Stalin aided this movement until his death, and some expected Georgi Malenkov as his chosen successor to respond to managerial pressures in the post-Stalin era.

But Malenkov's role was never to mature, for Khrushchev took away his post as Party First Secretary and Nikolai Bulganin eventually took over his role as Prime Minister. The Central Committee of the Trade Union Council ordered revitalization of the moribund factory production conference in September, 1955, although it was not to interfere with the one-man management concept.[30] By statute of July 15, 1958, this conference was increased in power,[31] and the administration of a factory was required to seek agreement with the trade union on the dismissal of workers, conditions of work, wages, and the arrangement of shifts.

Further control over plant directors was instituted by the Communist Party in a resolution of June 26, 1959,[32] establishing a commission of control in the factory Party committees. A few days later Khrushchev demanded Party control over directors, and an order followed within ten days approving a set of regulations on Party control.[33] It was evident that the specter of industrial tsars beyond the reach of both party and trade union had been perceived, and steps had been taken to halt the trend.

Kosygin's call in 1965 for expansion of the personal responsibility of managers must be read against this record. What can be expected as consequences? Clearly the central committee of the Trade Union Council foresees danger, for its secretary announced that an increase in powers of the enterprise will require a strengthening in the responsibility of the trade unions, especially as to salaries and employment.[34] He did not mention the director by name, but it is to the director that the expanded powers are given under the enterprise statute. It is the director who has the responsibility to reduce costs, and the trade union chief seemed to be indicating fear that costs might be reduced by cutting the wage bill through dismissal of workers and rationalization of production, since under the new method of personnel planning, directors are instructed only as to the total wage fund available to them. Within that total they can increase or reduce the total number of employees as efficiency seems to require. Further, they can influence wage levels of individuals by overtime pay and bonus payments for outstanding production.

The trade union secretary, perhaps, had this possibility in mind when he emphasized the role of the union in distributing profits and establishing bonus regulations. But he also touched upon another feature of union structure when he urged that the trade union councils at regional levels be kept alive.[35] These councils had long existed to coordinate at each regional level (city, province, and republic) the work of trade unions structured along functional lines to parallel the management lines of Stalin's ministries. They had come to life under Khrushchev's economic regional system, for management was placed upon a regional basis. With return to the ministerial form of administration, the trade unions seemingly feared the end of their regional influence. They wanted to keep their Khrushchev role, perhaps because they could be far more influential politically when combined as a single source of trade union policy at each regional level than when divided between branches of the economy with a single coordinating center only at the very top, where they were clearly subject to control by supreme Party agencies.

Kosygin has probably anticipated danger in creating a strengthened source of political influence through granting new authority to the plant directors, for in Marxist analysis economic power makes for political power. Perhaps in an effort to convince his economic lieutenants of their duties to work with all, he told them, "But one-man management must be organizationally combined with the broadest participation of workers and employees in the discussion of the major questions of the economic life of the enterprise and the management of production. The success of an economic manager's work depends upon his reliance on the collective [the trade union], and upon the prestige he wins by his own high businesslike qualities and adherence to principles." [36] In short, good management requires that a manager be an able labor relations man.

If the 1965 reforms strengthen the potential of economic managers, do they also strengthen the voice of the unions as an interest group? The latter have one advantage over the managers in that they have an institution through which to express their views, and it was strengthened on the regional level during the Khrushchev period. For years they have been silent politically, for their politically oriented leader, Mikhail P. Tomsky, was silenced in 1929 by dismissal when he sought to continue the unions as a force against management, as had been the case under the New Economic Policy of the 1920's. At that time the trade unions became a state institution as administrator of factory safety regulations and social insurance to those injured but remaining on the job. Further, they performed a managerial function in exhorting workers to increased production.

Under the 1930 change, the trade unions steadily lost influence, until by 1937 they no longer concluded collective agreements with management and questions were raised as to whether they still had a function to perform. Only after the war, as a means of instilling strong labor discipline, did they revive and regain their function as negotiators with management, but the agreements they reached were little more than restatements of laws relating to labor and exhortations to the members to increase productivity. Their one normative role was to provide for distribution of bonuses to projects for which the workers had preference.

With the 1965 reforms Kosygin foresees new importance for the collective agreement, as a stimulus not only to workers' production but to management's efficient performance under the watchful eyes of a trade union intent upon controlling bureaucratic abuses, such as failure to introduce modern techniques and to innovate. "Every worker and employee of an enterprise must know what concrete steps will be taken to insure that the enterprise will operate better and more profitably." [37]

Checks and balances have been strengthened in the Soviet system, not as between executive, legislative, and judicial branches of government in the United States, but as between emerging social forces, and notably those whose prestige and power are destined to increase with expansion of production, if experience elsewhere is to be a guide.

Will this lead to expanding pluralism in Soviet society, or, at least, to an increase in the incipient pluralistic features already existing and publicly manifest in fields unrelated to the economic reforms, notably those of literature and art? Will a stratum of industrial managers and a revitalized trade union organization emerge to challenge the monolithic all-embracing leadership of the Communist Party?

That question is being put in many quarters outside the Soviet Union. Soviet authorities have indicated that they do not even want to discuss it in meetings of international scientific associations.[38] Yet, there are suggestions at home that the public is mindful of the possibilities. Lepeshkin informed the world in February, 1965, that hundreds of letters had been received by the Institute of Law asking why there were not several candidates proposed for seats as deputies to the various soviets, and he noted that "this is not a secondary question." [39] The same suggestion has since come from the Prime Minister of the Armenian Republic.

Multiple candidates may run only on their personal records, and probably this is what the Soviet leadership would expect if such an innovation were proposed; but would the movement stop at that? Experience elsewhere suggests that if there are several candidates for a post, they attract the support of various groups, which compete to attract votes to their favorite candidate. Factions are then created around the candidates. After nearly fifty years of experience with a one-party system, it is incredible that factions in the U.S.S.R. would take the form of multiple parties, but it is not incredible that they might attract the support of differing interests.

Perhaps because of these possibilities the Twenty-third Party Congress moved in the direction of re-establishing a smaller, more disciplined, elite Party removed from the administrative tasks placed upon it by Khrushchev's system. The Party wishes to raise the heads of its members above the horizon created by an administrative job and to reassert their ideological leadership as "generalists." Can it prevent the emergence of interest groups and perhaps even of politically organized factions? No doubt Party leaders think it can, but a study of comparative politics suggests that they will have a hard time if the present temper of the public of the U.S.S.R. continues to develop. The logic of economic development is intensification of varying interests and strengthening of various forces. If this logic is repeated in the U.S.S.R., the economic reforms of 1965 can be expected to have notable political consequences for which the Communist Party has sought to prepare, but with which it may be unable to cope.

IV

Convergence: Possibility and Probability

Peter Wiles

For this writer to write again of convergence is to engage in self-criticism. In an earlier work on the subject I was very sceptical about the possibility that the social and economic systems of the United States and the Soviet Union would spontaneously converge. Three different possibilities were listed: "The first may be called the strong case for convergence, and is based largely on predictions of American change: (1) that new rational methods of economic planning must eventually supersede both the free market and the arbitrary Stalinist system of *a priori* allocations. The other two are the weak case, and are based largely on predictions of Soviet change: (2) that reason must eventually triumph over dogma, or managers over ideologues, so as to make the policies of the leadership, if not similar, at least tolerant; and (3) that rich societies with a high level of mass consumption all tend to be, if not similar, again at least tolerant."[1] I still think that these are the main possibilities, but I have much more faith in them now than then.

To discuss convergence is to prophesy social and economic trends in *both* countries. The good prophet will list all possible pictures of the future and reduce them to those that are internally coherent. One can, at least, exclude some as self-contradictory, but that leaves open an almost infinite field which can be further limited only by extrapolation. Such extrapolation can be only from current trends, and my self-criticism is based solely on a change from the trends current in 1962 to those prevailing in 1966. It appeared sensible in 1962 to take the 1961 Party program seriously; today, following the fall of Khrushchev, it would be madness. It is the nature of a sensible prophet to change his mind from time to time; recent events *should* bulk very large. At the very least, the prophet who disregards current events must say why he is doing so.

Let us first, somewhat dogmatically, dispose of the future of United States society and its economy. This is comparatively simple, since few new trends have been observable between 1932 and 1962. States' rights and economic *laissez-faire* will be more and more eroded, the influence of the federal government increasing in both areas; but basically the United States economy will continue to be capitalist. Whatever the federal government's degree of influence and information, it will not set up a Soviet-type command economy; nor will the American economy follow the Yugoslav model. A genuine if very imperfect market will remain and will continue to be characterized by private ownership of the means of production (that is, profits will still be generated, and appropriated by private persons having a title to them other than employment). Moreover, most consumption will continue to be paid for privately: expenses for museums, education, Medicare, etc., will grow, but hardly as a percentage of the growing total of consumption. Though the very poor will benefit disproportionately from the growth of the welfare state, most personal incomes will continue to be decided by the market and accidents of inheritance. No great equalization appears to be in store, but since everyone will be richer, a still larger fraction of the population will own securities and major consumer durables. In short, it is sane to predict "more of the same" in every sphere.

In only two important respects must we predict things that barely seemed discernible in 1932. First, there will be much fuller employment than in the past, with or without a Vietnamese war. When the late President Kennedy accepted Keynesian budgeting in his speech at Yale on June 11, 1962, he indeed initiated a trend. As always, our prophecies rest on the assumption that there will be no major war. If Vietnam escalates to the point of absorbing a million United States troops, that, too, might be called a major war, shifting the social and economic scene too much for worthwhile prediction.

Second, we have to make some provision in our thinking about a veritable joker in the pack: civil rights. Whatever governments may do, it is wise to predict the continuing denial of equal treatment to Negroes by the white population at large. Endemic civil disorder and semi-racial crime are therefore a possibility that I take perhaps more seriously than many observers. I explicitly assume that such tensions will not mount so intolerably as to cause the election of an extreme right-wing President and Congress.

These two factors, the war in Vietnam and Negro civil rights, have no exact parallel in the U.S.S.R., but

I am uneasy about the role of national minorities concentrated in defined geopolitical areas in the U.S.S.R. Much more liberalization might lead these minorities to explode, again with consequences that cannot be predicted.

Turning to the U.S.S.R., which is our essential topic, let us take first the new and more rational methods of central planning. It is even clearer today than it was in 1962 that the centralized command economy, made perfectly rational by computers provided with all the information required, is a thing of the far future. Not only is information still simply unavailable but the computers still would take an almost infinitely long time to process this information if it were available, and then with great probability of gross error. We may confidently anticipate that computation time will soon be reduced radically, but data collection has no such glorious future. It hardly seems possible to collect the necessary data as punctually as necessary and in the quantity needed; to say nothing of the required accuracy, since a very small initial error may lead to staggering errors in the computers' results.

But one day the centrally computed, detailed command economy will be practicable, that is, its administrative cost will have fallen to about that of a market economy. There is even now a multiplicity of minor business uses, reaching right up into such large aggregates as the United States Department of Defense. One day there will be a choice of alternative ways of running the whole economy rationally. There might, for instance, be absolute *laissez-faire,* total centralization, or innumerable compromises. We might centralize investment alone, leaving consumption to the market, or industry as opposed to agriculture, or government departments and public corporations as against the private sector, etc. Most of these choices are open equally to the United States and the U.S.S.R. Abram Bergson, for instance, has pointed out to me that private enterprise might find it profitable to have its decisions centrally computed, and thus set up a voluntary center of its own.

We may be sure that the United States will make a much more decentralized use of computers than the U.S.S.R., which has all along preferred an irrational centralization (worked out on the backs of envelopes), and will continue to favor something more centralized. In particular, this fits with the lingering Marxist suspicion of money. Money, this ideology still holds, should be abolished, yet rationality, say modern Marxists, must be strengthened. As I wrote in 1962, in a passage for which I do not now repent: "Clearly, the 'electronic market' is a *deus ex machina,* strengthening rationality at the very same time as abolishing ordinary money. One can of course object that the variables in the equations are prices, since they fulfill exactly the same function. But any faithful Marxist anxious to abolish money in accordance with prophecy and yet to economise resources, is entitled to this semantic loophole. Money, he will say, is the folding stuff; what makes computer relays click isn't money."

But at present, and this is where I erred before, the new pursuit of economic rationality in the Soviet Union dictates decentralization. There must be considerably more freedom for the enterprise, more competition, and fewer arbitrary prices than at present. At the same time the pursuit of full employment and monopoly control in the United States dictates an increase of powers at the center. Therefore, however different the ultimate intentions as to the uses of computation, the immediate prospect is undoubtedly one of some slight convergence in the relative roles of government and enterprise in both countries. It was a bold prophecy indeed, and surely a false one, that I made in 1962: ". . . major ideological pronouncements, and such basic measures as the amalgamation of *kolkhozy* and their subjection to ever more outside interference, show which way the wind really is blowing. The reverse movement in the rights of managers and the choice of indicators is a temporary reaction to

Stalin's too hasty centralization. It is a prudent, tactical retreat towards semi-market methods in order to introduce a little rationality here and now. It is merely *reculer pour mieux sauter;* as in all other fields communist strategic aims remain true to the classics of Marxism-Leninism, and tactical deviations must not blind us to this." But this underestimates the majestic extent of the present decentralization and its likely effect on ideology. *Per contra,* of course, the ultimate victory of the computer over the market, if it comes, will have a devastating effect on United States ideology.

Just how much attention should be paid any more to Communist long-term or ideological aims? It seems to me that Lenin and Khrushchev were very closely bound to them; that in particular Khrushchev, a pragmatist and no intellectual, had a simple and unquestioning faith in such parts of the orthodoxy as he understood—and governed the country accordingly. This was surprisingly often possible, and it came out in many details. Stalin's cynicism did not abolish such faith, but merely drove it, like everything else, underground. He did not bring about the End of Ideology, any more than he uprooted, say, poetry or genetic research. He simply froze the Soviet mind, so that when the thaw came one of the crocuses was indeed a genuine ideological enthusiasm. The End of Ideology appears to be coming now, only after the Khrushchev period, when the practical problems and theoretical contradictions have been more frankly discussed.

Already under Khrushchev a shrewd observer might have seen the beginning of the End of Ideology. For, as Zbigniew Brzezinski has pointed out, "the ruling body now contained at least one professional specialist in ideological matters." [2] Lenin was his own ideologist. Stalin, no intellectual, had briefly suffered, and then disposed of, Nikolai Bukharin. Khrushchev, no worse educated or more pragmatic than Stalin, had to have Mikhail Suslov. It was as if John XXIII were Pope, while Cardinal Ottaviani wrote the dogma. All the great Communist leaders—Lenin, Stalin, Mao, Tito—have been their own Popes, and very rightly. For in an ideological dictatorship, where so much is an article of faith, the role of definer of the faith is charismatic. If the dictator does not himself define it, he loses his charisma for not doing his job (like an African tribal king who can't make rain), and the ideology loses its charisma because it is handed over, like foreign policy or industrial management, to some subordinate. So far, Stalin has been the only second-generation Communist dictator to combine the charisma of faith-definer with that of power-wielder. In China Lin Piao may succeed for a while; but it stretches the imagination that this should ever happen again in the U.S.S.R. Therefore, ideology will play a much more subordinate role than in the past.

Even apart from this, Brezhnev and Kosygin are very different characters from Khrushchev; nor is this chance, since the times demand it. They are not simple men, and the simplicity of the previous leaders is a very important point. One can be very sly in practical ways, as peasants are sly, without being attracted to new ideas. Both Stalin and Khrushchev were thus sly. It requires a simple and indeed a sly man to believe in 1960 in an ideology formulated in 1860, but the new leaders are not self-taught. Of course it matters what subjects they were taught: far from being intellectuals, they are both technicians. They have no more interest in or sympathy for art and literature than their predecessors, but they do have a new-found devotion to social science which will surely shake communism to its base.

The rise of social science is an immense component in, virtually the definition of, the End of Ideology. An ideology is a systematic faith, secular or theistic, upon which one bases one's social, political, and—normally—economic behavior. It contains, of course, empirical propositions, but many of them are false. They may have been false from the very beginning, like the labor theory of value, or they may have become false with the passage of time, like the denial that a capitalist welfare state is possible. For the rest, the whole system may or may not be coherent and may or may not be a true interpretation of what the founder said. The effect of social science upon such a social faith is to point out that some of the empirical propositions are false; that some of the propositions of whatever kind do not agree with each other; and that the founder didn't mean that, anyway. Moreover, these days the social sciences are extremely complicated and professional. No wonder, then, that party *apparatchiki* have always insisted upon the simplest possible methodology; busy people, concerned with governing, have no time for mere professionalism. But the social sciences cannot grow under such control. To make their full contribution they must pass, and have passed, well beyond the understanding of the Party member in the street.

Therefore, the claim of Marxism to incorporate, to subsume, indeed to *be,* all the social sciences is completely indispensable if it is to be a functioning ideology. The *raison d'être* of the Party is that it possesses a truth that others can learn only from it, and has also the monopoly of changing and interpreting that truth. The new independence of sociology, economics, and management studies, the new sophistication and especially mathematization of techniques in these fields, threaten this position in many ways. First, the truth is now to be obtained by free inquiry, and so not in the old manner of biblical exegesis and deference to political authority. Second, the truth is very complicated, so that the authorities cannot understand it when it has been discovered. Their role will be simply to implement it. Third, there is only one truth, which a "capitalist" social scientist also can discover, and, all too embarrassingly, often has already discovered.

We may compare the very similar situation in the arts. It is a primary tenet of communism that there should be only one level, only one "height of brow" in the arts. Everybody must be at least able to understand and like everything. Nominally, this doctrine is enunciated in favor of the proletariat, for whom the arts are written, composed, painted, performed. In fact, it facilitates Party control: an *apparatchik*, of all human beings, is the least likely to savor or understand an artistic innovation. For his own convenience, the censor keeps both form and content simple and traditional. The arts have been more or less controlled from 1906, when Lenin insisted on loyalty in Party writers, until the present day. The attempt to control the natural sciences has been less obviously necessary, less permanent, and less successful. It began about 1925 and ended about 1954. But it is the social sciences that are the keep of the castle. They have been controlled since Marx became a Marxist. It was to deviants in this field alone that *he* showed dictatorial intolerance. Yet they are now so practically useful that they are being emancipated.

All this spells, to my mind, *convergence*. No ideology can withstand a free search for truth, and in the long run what people think determines what they do, whether or not other pragmatic considerations have determined what they think in the first place. The divergence since 1917 was basically ideological, and so now will be the convergence.

In the field of economics the End of Ideology is quite specially marked. Thus, during the New Economic Policy there was a market and extreme decentralization, but these were seen as a tactical retreat alone. There was no suggestion that such things were appropriate to full communism, or even to socialism: the very name of a socialist state was refused to the U.S.S.R. by its own rulers. The most right-wing among them, Bukharin, continued to think of socialism as a centralized, publicly owned, command economy. Today, on the contrary, independent economic thought is held to be useful to the state, and the basic ideological revision has been made that "commodity turnover" is compatible with socialism. Khrushchev was tone deaf to such matters. It is probable, for instance, that the names of Liberman and Kantorovich never occurred in any of his numerous and lengthy public speeches. He was not in the slightest degree interested in revisionist economics.

In particular, can we continue to have faith in Marxism if we no longer believe in the labor theory of value? Marx, after all, thought it was the basis of his system; but its evident falsity has at last won wide, if tacit, acceptance. A two-part answer seems correct. Marxism as a state religion is on the way out in any case; the building will fall down whether the foundation stone cracks or not. But second, the labor theory of value is not an important part of Leninism, of the ideology of seizing and maintaining power through a special Party; nor, curiously enough, of Stalinist thinking on how to run a socialist economy. An ordinary Party member certainly could not answer simple questions on the labor theory of value.

The theory has not prevented calculation in money, and decision by profit in some cases, ever since 1928; nor the payment of interest on savings accounts; nor much else that Marx condemned. All it has done is cloud thinking, and prevent some reforms. It has, for instance, ensured that until 1966 no interest be charged on enterprise capital derived from the budget (but not the bank!); that there be no land rent paid;

that the price mechanism be eschewed *on the whole;* etc.

It is said that there is far more Biblical evidence for a personal devil than for the Virgin Birth. Yet disbelief in the former is almost required, while doubt as to the latter is still apt to cause scandal. It is the same with all great established faiths: we choose, or have chosen for us, which articles we really believe in; we do not demand intellectual consistency of ourselves in such matters. Marxism without the labor theory of value is entirely possible.

The End of Ideology has its administrative counterpart in Managerial Revolution, which I define as "the onset of a reasonable professionalism." [3] Khrushchev struggled against this trend, reorganizing and re-reorganizing Party and state. His view was that Party *apparatchiki* must always be in an administrative position to dominate state officials. It would be meaningless to speak of a convergence between the two economic systems while one of them consisted of two parallel hierarchies of command. Our neglect of the direct role of the Party in the economy is a major scandal of Sovietology, and no defense is needed if we here go into it at some length.

Before Khrushchev, there had been much discussion of this role. It had been greater and smaller at one time or another, and many different schemes had

oblast' boundaries, and thus very greatly enhanced the power and prestige of *oblast'* Party secretaries. The great state officials like the minister of nonferrous metallurgy disappeared, and there was for a short time no state official more influential than these Party prefects. They could, of course, easily dominate their local *sovnarkhoz* chairman.

Carried to its extreme, Khrushchevism would have simply converted the Party into a substitute for the state, performing all its functions and liable itself to the Managerial Revolution as here defined. But Khrushchev's intentions, though probably self-contradictory, fell short of that. He wanted a detailed command economy with plans worked out more at the local level and no bureaucracy. The Party was to dominate but not supplant the state. But the scheme proved technically unworkable. Much of what the ministries had previously done could not be devolved upon the *sovnarkhozy;* it had to be done in Moscow, so the task was loaded onto the central planning organ or onto new state committees sitting in Moscow. Moreover, the *sovnarkhozy* proved unworkably small, and had to be amalgamated; which destroyed the parallelism with the *oblast'* and so diminished the powers of the *oblast'* Party secretary.

If Khrushchev had been Tito and abolished the central command economy out of hand, it might have been different. But he was not, and the logic of that economy reasserted itself inexorably until we now have again great central ministries and no *sovnarkhozy* at all. Furthermore, the growth of enterprise independence surely will never render these organs superfluous; there will always be a command economy of sorts. As to the *oblast'* Party secretary, he is back where he was in 1956, and is indeed warned against detailed interference. It would seem that managers *must* take over such an economy: the Party cannot be influential except at the very top, where politicians decide policy as in any other country, and at the very bottom, where it is the business of Communists to ensure labor morale. This applies even to agriculture, which was always a special case. So much was Soviet agriculture used to being under the thumb of local Party officials that Khrushchev did not bother to subject it to the *sovnarkhozy* in 1957; these were a "punishment" for the managerialized sectors of industry and construction, while the agricultural chain of command was from his point of view satisfactory already. But now, perhaps for the first time since collectivization, we see a solid state machine growing up in agriculture, too.

Truth to tell, the smoother things run and the more established the system is the less need there is of *préfets*. The center makes fewer planning mistakes, communications are better, the population is more docile, and experts are more numerous; so local crises are simply less common. Without crises, the middle layers of the Party lose one whole function. The Party's grip on *nomenklatura* is still very tight, and it is still the most effective local lobbyist for budgetary funds. These are very important matters indeed, but even here the Party is insecure. *Nomenklatura* is giving way to ever more stringent requirements that candidates be technically educated; central funds are allocated by ever more rational economic principles that work automatically. Even though today these remain essentially Party matters, the power of the Party in the economy is past its Khrushchevian peak.

That ministers and enterprise managers should be Party members, indeed increasingly so, is both certain and irrelevant. For the Party is not merely a freemasonry lodged in an alien structure, but a church, a structure on its own with a current line of its own which it has endeavored successfully to enforce. Professionals and technocrats who belong to it are indeed "freemasons." The laity may resent their cohesion and their tendency to promote each other, but *they* are not a parallel government. Moreover, they are not through-and-through Communists, but conformists who have found membership necessary for their careers. The parallel government is that of the full-time *apparatchiki,* who can easily mobilize the "secular" Party members. It is, however, the very existence of such secular members, growing in numbers and expertise, that gives the state machine independent weight, making the middle ranks of the Party fifth wheels on the economic coach. The difference between the Twenty-second (1962) and the Twenty-third (1966) Party Congresses shows most of this very clearly. The very liturgy is different. Thus Khrushchev in 1962 ended his great speech in the standard way with the word "Communism"—meaning the future utopia called in the West full communism: "Forward, to the victory of Communism." In 1966 Brezhnev did the same, and this is what he said: "Long live Communism."

It is almost as if the bare faith had replaced the actual pilgrimage. Moreover, the emphasis on this subject was immeasurably greater in the body of Khrushchev's speech than in Brezhnev's. Again both Congresses were insistent on economic rationality, but the second much more so, and only in the second was the dread phrase "social science" on everybody's lips. There is even a most un-Khrushchevian reference to the strengthening of the state.

Moreover, to turn to our third avenue of Convergence, collective consumption [5] received a severe blow at the Twenty-third Congress. Khrushchev and the 1961 Party program promised that by 1981 more than half of personal consumption would be collective. In particular, the private car, symbol of inefficient and anarchic United States individualism, would be discouraged in favor of car hire. It is difficult to exaggerate the importance of the private car in Communist countries. Families scrape and save and intrigue for it; professors take jobs abroad and live off bread and water to bring back a Volkswagen; black marketeers acquire small trucks that are legally to be supplied only to enterprises. Once a car is acquired, its owner faces infinite difficulties in regard to repairs and even in getting gasoline. Let the planners once decide to satisfy the demand for private cars, and they have opened the Pandora's box of road construction, traffic control, parking problems and all. At no point is it clearer that Communist dialectical materialism has, correctly understood, no connection with capitalist Philistine materialism. Consumer's sovereignty is no part of the doctrine; self-sacrifice and discipline are.

Seeing all this clearly—or does he see it clearly?—Kosygin has made the most fateful of all promises: to raise personal vehicle production about fourfold from 1965 to 1970, as opposed to less than twofold in the previous five years. On the future of collective consumption generally, Kosygin promises to raise it by 40 per cent during this Five-Year Plan, the same increase as for money wages. In the previous seven years, under Khrushchev, it increased much more rapidly, shifting proportions considerably. Thus in 1957, the proportion of the social wage to the privately paid out wage was 26.6 per cent; in 1964 it was 34.5 per cent; in 1970 it is planned to be 35 per cent.

Does all this amount to capitalism? My answer must take into account not only all that has been said above but the decentralization and rationalization described by Mr. Bergson. It is a firm but moderate No. Allow, for instance, that profit is a criterion of what to produce. Profit can always be a criterion without being an incentive. But, in fact, the Soviet-type economies are moving towards profit, not merely as a criterion but also as an incentive. In the future, there will be fewer plan fulfillment bonuses and it will be more a question of one's bonus coming out of the profit that one's enterprise is making.

How, under such a system, does the manager differ from a capitalist? He has an enterprise; he aims to make profit; the more profit he makes the greater his income; he makes lawful decisions without reference to a higher body. Is that capitalism? It is, of course, a semantic matter.

Property, we say in the West in our sophisticated way, is a meaningless word. Property is a bundle of all types of particular rights: the right to set the price, the right to define the output, the right to keep the profit, the right to fire, etc. And, of course, any of these rights may be concentrated to a greater or lesser extent in some higher authority. A capitalist enterprise may be subjected to price control. It may lose its right to hire or fire, which may have been taken over by the trade unions. Innumerable rights have, in fact, been taken over by somebody else, so that the word property has become rather meaningless. We should ask only: "Who has which right, if any?" This is a complicated question, to which no one answer can be given.

But there is at least one right inherent by definition in private property: the right to sell the thing that I own. Private property in the means of production implies not only that I can sell the individual means—a machine, a building, the work in progress—but also the whole enterprise as a going concern: nay more, I can sell the right to a part of the profits while retaining the right to the rest. We thus arrive at the *equity share,* the real core of the capitalist system. Under all forms of Communism—Yugoslav and even Soviet—an enterprise may incur a fixed debt, but that is not the same thing as an equity share. The enterprise owes a certain sum to, say, a bank from which it has borrowed at short term. It may pay interest on this; now it must even pay interest on sums allocated to it at long term by the treasury. In Yugoslavia, where there are many banks and other lenders of money, the original creditor can even resell the enterprise's debt to another lender, if he is pressed for cash. Thus the whole capitalist market in bills and bonds has been reproduced, and the same might well happen shortly in the most decentralized of soviet-type economies, say Czechoslovakia.

But this is very far indeed from reestablishing capitalism, since a debt at fixed interest conveys no right to share in the profit, and no right of control. That a socialist enterprise should have a debt is banal; that the socialist creditor should resell the debt to another socialist creditor ought to be equally banal, a technical matter. But that a private person, not himself a manager, should have a right to the profit is revolutionary. I do not believe that equity shares will ever come into existence, even in the Yugoslav system. (It is conceivable that *public* authorities should own shares in Yugoslav enterprises, and that *private* savers should buy an enterprise's fixed debt. The former situation would especially come about when enterprises and consumers formed consortia to found new enterprises. The latter situation might look bad but would be little less socialistic than the already universal private savings deposits.) Therefore, I believe, there always will be grounds for calling one system socialist and the other capitalist.

But, after all, this is a rather narrow distinction. There are so many other reforms and potential similarities that the single difference on which I have insisted would seem to be of little importance. The Marxist labor theory of value is no longer regarded as fully valid; there are now charges on capital, and possibly there soon will be charges on land in order to allocate scarce resources rationally. Consumer's sovereignty has been directly recognized, and the plan has to be currently, not once a year, readjusted to take account of their wishes. The idea has been abandoned that the shape of buttons to be produced in Irkutsk has to be fixed in Moscow.

A less intellectual but surely just as important subject is the genuine revival of small capitalism. To run a seaside boardinghouse, to do a little tailoring at home, or to grow flowers seem unimportant to intellectuals, for whom economics is about steelmaking or the cultivation of wheat. But much money can be made out of flowers. A few years ago such activities, though legal, were subject to every sort of chicanery; though, curiously, no turnover taxes were levied on them. But they have apparently come to stay, and are now tolerated more than ever before. If we include agriculture, no less than 60 per cent of "socialist" Yugoslavia's force is made up of private entrepreneurs or the employees of private enterprise. In Poland the figure is little less. Non-agricultural private enterprise is very large in all Communist countries. Much of it is illegal and much only semi-legal; official statistics are worthless here. Even where agriculture is collectivized, notably in the U.S.S.R. and China, the actual decision-making and accounting unit is often so small in rural circumstances as to constitute only two families. I refer to the Chinese production team, prevalent now all over China, and to the Soviet "link," which is still a minority movement, especially strong in Kazakhstan.

The expansion of this sector is significant. It cannot be *meant* to last, but who knows? *Il n'y a que le provisoire qui dure,* especially when it is extremely popular with consumers and producers alike. The breach of socialist morality is gross and evident, but the ideology may yet be twisted to sanctify the whole thing. I know many East European Communists who are privately very frank that the ideology should be so changed.

Is all this good or bad for peace? To answer this question is to step perhaps too far outside economics. Foreign policies "converged" already in 1925, when Stalin put the Comintern second to Socialism in One Country, thus adopting the same policy of pure self-interest that governs all other states. The reader may take what comfort he likes from that. In matters of culture and political constitution, the basic causes of the cold war, the stirrings of Soviet liberalism are, if unmistakable, faint. Yet economic convergence must be good in itself, and here surely, again my initial pessimism was wrong. It is true that similar social systems have often fought—no one hated a Chinese war lord as much as another Chinese war lord. But Chinese war lords were not converging—they had never diverged. Here, on the other hand, the U.S.S.R. and the United States have stood dogmatically for opposed social principles and are now converging, if only a little.

A Soviet Communist would object that all this skirts the main point: class war. Different classes are in charge in the United States and in the U.S.S.R., and nothing changes that. These classes are at war, so there will be no convergence. To this it is only necessary to reply that class differences are diminishing in the United States and have, up to date, increased since 1917 in the U.S.S.R. The convergence of the economic management systems and of living standards brings about a similarity of social structure. The fact that in one place there was once a social revolution and in the other not will soon be of merely historical interest. History closes over its own wounds. The sociology of occupations—a sort of non-Marxist "relations of production"—constrains every society.

On the other side, Bertram Wolfe would ask us to distinguish between "within-system changes" and "changes in the system of Communism," and to expect only the former.[6] It is true that optimism is always foolhardy, and every optimistic forecast about Soviet Communism has hitherto proved false. Nothing here should be taken as a prophecy that there will be no atomic wars or no new Daniel-Sinyavski trial, nor do I even deny that a straightforward general reversion to Stalinism is possible. But I do assert that if the first two events are unpredictable, the third is now grossly improbable. I further assert that Wolfe's distinction between "within-" and "without-system" is unusable. The leaders define what the system is, and they have made many radical changes. The Italian Communist Party advocates cultural freedom now, and has come close to blessing a multi-party democracy. The Yugoslav League of Communists has for fifteen years practiced a market economy, and is now establishing the rule of law. In Czechoslovak economics, in Polish culture, in Rumanian foreign policy, very convergent phenomena are also observable. Only the Chinese remain outside the stream, and they are more confident than any United States technocrat or liberal in prophesying Soviet Union-United States convergence. It is not written in heaven, then, that the U.S.S.R. will not one day make an irreparable move towards reason, truth, and freedom.

Notes

NOTES TO CHAPTER I

1 *Ekonomika promyshlennosti SSSR* (Moscow), 1956, p. 393.
2 Herbert Levine, "The Centralized Planning of Supply in Soviet Industry," United States Congress, Joint Economic Committee, *Comparisons of the United States and Soviet Economies* (Washington: Government Printing Office, 1959), Part I, pp. 151–176.
3 Karl Marx, *Critique of the Gotha Programme* (New York: International Publishers, 1933), pp. 26–32.
4 *Ibid.*, pp. 27–28.
5 *Ibid.*, pp. 83–90.
6 *Ibid.*, p. 29.
7 *Ibid.*, p. 31.
8 On Marxian theory of communism *vis-à-vis* socialism see: Alexander Balinky, "Has the Soviet Union Taken a Step

toward Communism?", *Social Research,* XXVIII, No. 1 (Spring, 1961), 1–14; "The Proclaimed Emergence of Communism in the U.S.S.R.," *Social Research,* XXVIII, No. 3 (Autumn, 1961), 261–282.

9 This is a position taken by Albert Parry in *The New Class Divided* (New York: Macmillan, 1966).

10 Albert Parry, "Russia's New Bourgeois Grows Fat," *New York Times Magazine,* June 5, 1966, p. 44.

11 Eli Ginzberg, "Psychology and Manpower Policy," *American Psychologist,* XXI, No. 6 (June, 1966), 549.

12 Gregory Grossman, "Notes for a Theory of the Command Economy," *Institute of International Studies: Slavic and East European Series,* Reprint No. 118 (Berkeley: University of California, October, 1963), p. 101.

NOTES TO CHAPTER II

1 *Pravda,* September 28, 1965.

2 Dismissals of workers presumably will still require, as they have since 1958, the consent of the trade union factory committee. Also, under the new charter for the enterprise promulgated by the Council of Ministers on October 4, 1965 (*Ekonomicheskaia gazeta,* No. 42 [October, 1965]), the director of the enterprise apparently will still have to observe some average wage scheduled for salaried workers, though the precise meaning of this constraint is not clear.

On enterprise management's authority generally under the new reform program, in addition to the new charter and Kosygin's report cited above, see the Central Committee resolution in *Pravda,* October 1, 1965, and discussions of the program in *Pravda,* October 29 and November 12, 1965; and *Ekonomicheskaia gazeta,* No. 47 (November, 1965), p. 10; No. 7 (February, 1966), pp. 31ff.; No. 13 (March, 1966), p. 29.

3 *Ekonomicheskaia gazeta,* No. 47 (November, 1965), p. 10.

4 In addition to sales to others, according to *Ekonomicheskaia gazeta,* No. 6 (February, 1966), p. 32, "realized production" includes transfers to the enterprise's own capital construction work and "nonindustrial economic activities." An example of the latter presumably would be a factory restaurant. The source cited is not entirely clear regarding the treatment of changes in inventories of finished goods, but the reform program derives its meaning in part from the fact that "realized production" represents output net of such inventory changes, and certainly this is so. "Realized production," therefore, is properly identified, as I have identified it here, with sales.

5 On the new incentive arrangements, see *Ekonomicheskaia gazeta,* No. 6 (February, 1966), p. 33; No. 7 (February, 1966), pp. 31–32; No. 8 (February, 1966), pp. 21–22; No. 11 (March, 1966), p. 23; P. Krylov *et al.*, "O poriadke i usloviakh perekhoda k novoi sisteme," *Planovoe khoziaistvo* (April, 1966), 55ff.

6 *Pravda,* September 28, 1965; November 12, 1965; *Ekonomicheskaia gazeta,* No. 6 (February, 1966), pp. 31ff.; Krylov *et al., Planovoe khoziaistvo* (April, 1966), 55ff.

7 *Pravda,* April 6, 1966. See also *Ekonomicheskaia gazeta,* No. 18 (May, 1966), p. 8.

8 For an informative survey of the 1964–65 experiment, though possibly one overstressing the resulting autonomy of enterprises, see United States Central Intelligence Agency, *An Evaluation of Experimental Economic Reforms in the Consumer Industries of the USSR* (Processed), December, 1965.

9 That the measures on which I have focused have the effect of decentralizing authority in some degree is evident, but a question might be raised whether the reorganization referred to at the outset did not have a contrary effect. Thus, since branch ministries were often located in Moscow, did not the supplanting of these agencies by regional authorities

under Khrushchev's reorganization of May, 1957, represent a form of decentralization? And by the same token, does not the reestablishment of the branch-ministerial system now mean recentralization? Khrushchev's reorganization has sometimes been construed in the manner suggested, and perhaps with some basis, but the reorganization was quite complex and any shift in authority from Moscow must have been relatively limited. The current sequel to Khrushchev's reorganization is still too new to be fully understood, but the recentralization resulting from the abandonment of Khrushchev's regional authorities would also have to be limited. In any event, shifts in the locus of authority resulting from either the May, 1957, reorganization or its current abandonment occur only among superior agencies, and other reforms on which I have focused, under which authority is now transferred in a limited degree down to the enterprise, would seem decidedly more significant economically. On the reorganization of May, 1957, see Oleg Hoeffding, "Soviet Industrial Reorganization of 1957," *American Economic Review,* No. 2 (May, 1959); Abram Bergson, *The Economics of Soviet Planning* (New Haven: Yale University Press, 1964), Ch. 3. On the current change, see *Pravda,* October 3, 1965.

10 *The Economist,* March 19, 1966, p. 1100.

11 A. Birman, *Current Digest of the Soviet Press* (April 13, 1966), Part II, p. 3.

12 E. Lokshin, *CDSP* (May 3, 1961), p. 19; cited in Bergson, p. 156.

13 *Pravda,* January 11, 1965.

14 Joseph Berliner, *Factory and Manager in the USSR* (Cambridge, 1957); Bergson, pp. 72ff., 287ff.; Leon Smolinski, "The Soviet Economy," *Survey* (April, 1966), p. 94.

15 Bergson, Ch. 8.

16 Smolinski, p. 90.

17 *Ibid.,* p. 93.

18 Khrushchev, in *CDSP* (December 19, 1962), p. 9; Leonid Brezhnev, in *Pravda,* March 30, 1966.

19 Kosygin, in *Pravda,* December 10, 1964.

20 *Economic Problems of Socialism* (New York: International Publishers, 1952), p. 55.

21 On the more recent currents in Soviet economic thought see Marshall Goldman, "Economic Controversy in the Soviet Union," *Foreign Affairs* (April, 1963).

22 For Soviet official data, see Tsentral'noe statisticheskoe upravlenie, *Narodnoe khoziaistvo v 1964 g.* (Moscow, 1965), p. 575; *Pravda,* February 3, 1966. Western rates through 1962–63 from Joint Economic Committee, Congress of the United States, *Current Economic Indicators for the U.S.S.R.* (Washington, 1965), pp. 12, 13; and for 1963–65, from United States Department of State, "U.S.S.R. Falters in Economic Growth Race with the United States," release of September, 1965. For 1958–63, State Department estimates are slightly below those issued by the Joint Committee. Western data refer to the gross national product, as usually understood, while the Soviet figures refer to the net material product, as this is construed in Soviet usage. Regarding growth rates for the period covered, the difference in concept should not be important.

23 Abram Bergson, "The Great Economic Race: U.S.S.R. versus U.S.A.," *Challenge* (March, 1963); A. Nove, "Soviet Economic Progress," *Lloyds Bank Review* (October, 1965).

24 Bergson, "The Great Economic Race: U.S.S.R. versus U.S.A.," p. 5.

25 *Pravda,* September 28, 1965.

26 Whether the oil supply base and its customers operated under the new planning procedures is not clear, but apparently enterprises functioning under such procedures have had similar experiences. On the experience with the reforms to date, see CIA, *An Evaluation of Experimental Economic Reforms in the U.S.S.R.; CDSP* (February 23, 1966), pp.

25–26; (April 6, 1966), p. 29; *Pravda,* January 19, 1966, March 9, 1966, April 20, 1966; *Pravda Ukrainy,* March 18, 1966; *Soviet Studies, Information Supplement,* July, 1965, p. 11; January, 1960, pp. 23, 30; *Ekonomicheskaia gazeta,* No. 11 (March, 1966), pp. 21, 26–28; No. 15 (April, 1966), p. 36; No. 16 (April, 1966), p. 29; No. 17 (April, 1966), pp. 15–17; No. 18 (May, 1966), p. 8; No. 19 (May, 1966), p. 19.

27 On recent developments in the use of mathematical economics and advanced computers in the U.S.S.R., and the possible economic impact of such developments, see *Mathematics and Computers in Soviet Economic Planning* (New Haven, forthcoming); and Egon Neuberger, "Libermanism, Computopia and Visible Hand," *American Economic Review,* No. 2 (May, 1966). The expression "visible hand," which I use earlier, first came to my notice in Neuberger's article, but Neuberger (p. 132, n. 1) points out that the expression had been used previously by Joseph Berliner.

NOTES TO CHAPTER III

1 V. I. Lenin, *Sochinenia,* XXVII (3rd ed.; Moscow, 1928–1937), p. 252.

2 I. I. Evtikhiev and V. A. Vlasov, *Administrativnoe pravo* (Moscow, 1946), p. 6.

3 Speech of September 27, 1965, to Central Committee of the Communist Party of the Soviet Union, in *Pravda,* September 28, 1965, p. 1; English translation in *Current Digest of the Soviet Press* (October 13, 1965), p. 4.

4 "Theses" stated to Central Committee of C.P.S.U., March 29, 1957, in *Pravda,* March 30, 1957; English translation in *CDSP* (May 8, 1957), p. 3; *Pravda,* May 8, 1957, p. 1; English translation in *CDSP* (June 12, 1957), p. 3; *Pravda,*

May 11, 1957; English translation in *CDSP* (June 12, 1957), p. 14.

5 Resolution of Central Committee of C.P.S.U., November 23, 1962, *Izvestia,* No. 279, November 24, 1962, p. 1. English translation in John N. Hazard, *The Soviet System of Government* (3rd ed.; New York, 1964), p. 261. Khrushchev speech of November 19, 1962, *Izvestia,* No. 275, November 20, 1962, p. 1.

6 V. Stepanov, *Izvestia,* December 19, 1962, p. 4; English translation in *CDSP* (January 16, 1963), p. 30.

7 "Fidelity to Leninist Organizational Principles," *Pravda,* November 18, 1964; English translation in *CDSP* (December 2, 1964), p. 3.

8 "The C.P.S.U. in Figures (1961–1964)," *Partinaia zhizn,* No. 10 (May, 1965), p. 8; English translation in *CDSP* (August 11, 1965), p. 14.

9 Resolution of Central Committee of C.P.S.U., November 16, 1964, in *Pravda,* November 17, 1964, p. 1; English translation in *CDSP* (December 2, 1964), p. 3.

10 "Exactingness Is an Important Feature of Party Guidance," *Partinaia zhizn,* No. 20 (October, 1964), p. 3; English translation in *CDSP* (November 11, 1964), pp. 4–5.

11 Leonard Schapiro, *The Government and Politics of the Soviet Union* (London, 1965), p. 83.

12 Alfred G. Meyer, *The Soviet Political System: An Interpretation* (New York, 1965), p. 113.

13 Speech of Leonid Brezhnev to Twenty-third Communist Party Congress, March 29, 1966, in *Pravda,* March 30, 1966; English translation in *CDSP,* Part I (April 13, 1966), p. 3.

14 Zbigniew Brzezinski, "The Soviet Political System: Transformation or Degeneration," *Problems of Communism,* XV (January-February, 1966), p. 1.

15 Speech of A. N. Kosygin to Central Committee of C.P.S.U., September 27, 1965, in *Pravda,* September 28, 1965; English translation in *CDSP* (October 13, 1965), pp. 3, 7.

16 *Ibid.*, p. 12. During the years between Stalin's death in 1953 and Khrushchev's reorganization of 1957 some of the all-union type ministries of Stalin's epoch were reorganized into union-republic type ministries (steel, nonferrous metallurgy, and coal), but the chemical and petroleum industries appeared as union-republic type ministries only after the reforms of 1965.
17 *Ibid.*
18 *Ibid.*, p. 13.
19 For an account of the process see J. A. Morrison, "Territorial-Administrative Structure of the U.S.S.R.," *American Quarterly on the Soviet Union,* I, No. 3 (October, 1938), pp. 25, 30–31.
20 Law of July 16, 1956, in *Pravda,* July 17, 1956, p. 2; English translation in *CDSP* (August 29, 1956), p. 15.
21 Decree of February 5, 1963, *Vedomosti Verkhovnogo Soveta,* No. 7 (1963), item 82.
22 A. I. Lepeshkin, "Burning Problems of Development in Soviet Public Law," *Sovetskoe Gosudarstvo i Pravo* (February, 1965), 5, 8; English translation in *CDSP* (April 28, 1965), pp. 3–4.
23 Decree of December 22, 1964, *Vedomosti Verkhovnogo Soveta,* No. 1 (1965), item 3.
24 *CDSP* (October 16, 1965), p. 7.
25 Lenin, *Sochinenia,* XXII (3rd ed.; Moscow, 1928–1937), p. 462; and XXIII, pp. 447, 450.
26 Resolution on the Tasks of Economic Construction, section 9, *VKP(b) v Rezoliutsiiakh i Resheniiakh S'ezdov, Konferentsii i Pelunmov Ts. K.*, Part I (Moscow, 1936), pp. 337, 341.
27 Resolution on the Work of Labor Unions, section 16 and section 20, *Ibid.*, Part II, pp. 60, 64–65.
28 J. V. Stalin, "Speech to First All-Union Conference of Workers in Socialist Industry," February 4, 1931, in *Problemy Leninizma* (10th ed.; Moscow, 1935), pp. 439, 444.
29 Order of September 5, 1929 in *Pravda,* September 7, 1929,

reprinted in L. Gintsburg, A. Kostel'tsev, and V. Khitev, *Sovetskoe khoziaistvennoe zakonodatel'stvo,* Part I (Moscow, 1934), p. 83.

30 Order of September 28, 1955, in E. V. Shorina, *Kollegial'nost i edinonachalie v sovetskom gosudarstvennom upravlenii* (Moscow, 1959).

31 *Vedomosti verkhovnogo soveta,* No. 15 (1958), item 282.

32 *Zapisnaia knizhka partiinogo aktivista* (Moscow, 1960), p. 149; English translation in John N. Hazard and Isaac Schapiro, *The Soviet Legal System* (Dobbs Ferry, N.Y., 1962), Part II, p. 95.

33 Order of July 12, 1959, in *Pravda,* July 13, 1959.

34 For analysis of this feature of change, see J. P. Saltiel, "La Réforme de la Gestion de l'Economie Soviétique," *Le Courrier des Pays de l'Est,* No. 40 (November 4, 1965), pp. 5, 44.

35 *Ibid.*

36 *CDSP* (October 13, 1965), p. 14.

37 *Ibid.,* p. 14.

38 V. Chkhikvadze and S. L. Zivs, "Comparative Law in the Practice of International Scientific Collaboration," *Sovetskoe gosudarstvo,* No. 2 (1966), pp. 12, 20.

39 A. N. Lepeshkin, p. 12.

NOTES TO CHAPTER IV

1 "Will Capitalism and Communism Spontaneously Converge?", *Encounter* (June, 1963), 84–90. This article was written in 1962.

2 "The Soviet Political System; Transformation or Degeneration," *Problems of Communism,* XV, No. 1 (January-February, 1966), 1–15.

3 This is of course a much less exciting concept than that of James Burham, who orginated the phrase. For him the

managers were a class with an ideology, consciously taking power.

4 This basic idea is due to Mr. Jerry Hough of the Harvard Russian Research Center.

5 The present list of items comprises kindergartens and nurseries; general and higher education; medicine; rest homes, spa treatments; cultural enlightenment, physical training, sport; housing, services and urban amenities; old people's homes. Nearly every one of these items can also be obtained privately, and in most cases the consumer has to pay some part of the cost (for example, for school textbooks and uniforms, and notably the very low rent of houses). Presumably Soviet statistics present the net state subsidy to the individual.

6 "The Durability of Despotism in the Soviet System," address at St. Antony's College, Oxford University, June 1957.

Bibliography

Balinky, Alexander. "The Proclaimed Emergence of Communism in the U.S.S.R.," *Social Research*, XXVIII, No. 2 (Autumn, 1961), 261–282.

Bergson, Abram. *The Economics of Soviet Planning*. New Haven: Yale University Press, 1964.

Berliner, Joseph. "Marxism and the Soviet Economy," *Problems of Communism*, XIII, No. 5 (September-October, 1964), 1–11.

Bornstein, Morris. "The Soviet Price Reform Discussion," *Quarterly Journal of Economics*, LXXVIII, No. 1 (February, 1964), 15–48.

Brzezinski, Zbigniew. "The Soviet Political System: Transformation or Degeneration," *Problems of Communism*, XV, No. 1 (January-February, 1966), 1–15.

Campell, Robert. "Marx, Kantorovich, and Movozhilov: *Stoimost'* versus Reality," *Slavic Review,* XX, No. 3 (October, 1961), 402–418.

Goldman, Marshall. "Economic Controversy in the Soviet Union," *Foreign Affairs,* XLI, No. 3 (April, 1963), 498–512.

Grossman, Gregory. "Notes for a Theory of the Command Economy," *Institute of International Studies: Slavic and East European Series,* Reprint No. 118, Berkeley: University of California, October, 1963.

Hazard, John. *The Soviet System of Government,* 3rd ed. Chicago: Chicago University Press, 1964.

Levine, Herbert. "Recent Developments in the Soviet Economy," *Aste Bulletin,* VII, No. 3 (Winter, 1965), 5–10.

Liberman, Yevsei. "The Plan, Profits and Bonuses," *Pravda,* September 9, 1962. Translated in *The Current Digest of the Soviet Press,* XIV, No. 36 (October 3, 1962), 13–15.

———. "The Plan, Profits, and Bonuses: A Reply to Critics," *Ekonomicheskaia gazeta,* November 10, 1962. Translated in *The Current Digest of the Soviet Press,* XIV, No. 45 (December 5, 1962), 17–19.

Marx, Karl. *Critique of the Gotha Programme.* New York: International Publishers, 1933.

Neuberger, Egon. "Libermanism, Computopia and Visible Hand," *American Economic Review, Proceedings,* LVI, No. 2 (May, 1966), 131–144.

Nove, Alec. *Economic Rationality and Soviet Politics: Was Stalin Really Necessary?* New York: Praeger, 1964.

———. "The Liberman Proposals," *Survey,* No. 47 (April, 1963), 112–118.

Parry, Albert. *The New Class Divided.* New York: Macmillan, 1966.

Prybyla, Jan. "The Convergence of Western and Communist Economic Systems: A Critical Estimate," *Russian Review,* XXIII, No. 1 (January, 1964), 3–17.

Robinson, Joan. "Consumer Sovereignty in a Planned Economy," in Anniversary Committee of the Polish Scientific Publishers Association (ed.), *On Political Economy and Econometrics,* II, *Essays in Honor of Oskar Lange.* New York: Pergamon Press, 1966.

Shaffer, Harry. "What Price Economic Reforms? Ills and Remedies," *Problems of Communism,* XII, No. 3 (May-June, 1963), 18–26.

Spulber, Nicolas. "Communism Tries the Profit System," *Challenge* (January-February, 1966), 10–11, 36, 39.

Tinbergen, Jan. "Do Communist and Free Economies Show a Converging Pattern?" *Soviet Studies,* XII, No. 4 (April, 1961), 331–341.

Treml, Vladimir. "Soviet Economics in Flux," *Aste Bulletin,* VI, No. 3 (Winter, 1964), 2–8.

United States Central Intelligence Agency. *An Evaluation of Experimental Economic Reforms in the Con-*

sumer Industries of the U.S.S.R. (Processed), December, 1965.

United States Congress, Joint Economic Committee, Subcommittee on Foreign Economic Policy. *New Directions in the Soviet Economy:* Part I, *Economic Policy;* Part IIA, *Economic Performance;* Part IIB, *Economic Performance;* Part III, *Human Resources;* Part IV, *The World Outside.* Washington: Government Printing Office, 1966.

Wiles, Peter. *The Political Economy of Communism,* Cambridge: Harvard University Press, 1962.

Zauberman, Alfred. "Liberman's Rules of the Game for Soviet Industry," *Slavic Review,* XXII, No. 4 (December, 1963), 734–744.